NORTH CAROLINA SLAVES
AND
FREE PERSONS OF COLOR

MECKLENBURG, GASTON, AND UNION COUNTIES

William L. Byrd, III
and John H. Smith

HERITAGE BOOKS
2007

HERITAGE BOOKS
AN IMPRINT OF HERITAGE BOOKS, INC.

Books, CDs, and more—Worldwide

For our listing of thousands of titles see our website
at
www.HeritageBooks.com

Published 2007 by
HERITAGE BOOKS, INC.
Publishing Division
65 East Main Street
Westminster, Maryland 21157-5026

International Standard Book Number: 978-0-7884-1851-8

For Evelyn Rhodes

Contents

Introduction

The records in this book were transcribed from original papers located in the North Carolina State Archives. Most of these papers are listed under general headings such as "Slaves and Free Negroes," or "Slaves and Free Persons of Color." Occasionally they are listed under the heading of "Miscellaneous Records."[1]

This particular group of papers were selected from the North Carolina counties of Mecklenburg, Gaston and Union. Not a few of these records are torn and faded. In some cases, part of the original text is missing, and many of the names of individuals are almost indecipherable.

---

[1] Thornton W. Mitchell, "Preliminary Guide to Records Relating to Blacks in the North Carolina State Archives," *Archives Information Circular* 17(June 1980): 3-4.

Nevertheless, every attempt has been made to transcribe these papers as accurately as possible.

Included are a plethora of civil and criminal actions pertaining to slaves and free persons of color. The interactions between both Blacks and Whites are displayed on an antagonistic and intimate level, and are dramatically played out through crime and punishment. The criminal cases are filled with intrigue involving murder, felonies, trading with slaves and harboring slaves.

The different sections of this book are broken down into the following categories: Division of Slaves, Civil Actions, Criminal Actions, Free Persons of Color, Hiring of Slaves, Petition Ex Parte, Sales of Slaves, and Coroner's Inquests. In addition to these categories are papers relating directly to white persons. These papers are broken down into the following categories: Sheriff's Vouchers, Lands Sold for Taxes, Return of Strays, Tax Receipts, Real Estate Valuations, Vendue Lists, Confederate Special Exemptions, Tax Delinquent Lists, and Tax Lists spanning the years 1763 to 1844. These categories are part of the Mecklenburg papers.

A table of cases has been provided at the back of the book along with a glossary of legal terms used in these papers. The definitions are derived from Black's Law Dictionary.

Mecklenburg County was formed in 1762 from Anson County by act of the General Assembly of the State of North Carolina. This act became effective February 1st 1763. It was named in honor of Princess Charlotte of Mecklenburg, the Queen of George III who was King of England. It is bounded by the State of South Carolina and Gaston, Lincoln, Iredell, Cabarrus and Union counties. Tryon County was formed in 1768 from Mecklenburgh, and Cabarrus was formed in 1792 from Mecklenburgh. Part of Mecklenburg was annexed to Cabarrus in 1794 and again in 1804. In 1842 Union County was formed from Anson and Mecklenburg.[2]

Gaston County was formed in 1846 from Lincoln County. It was named in honor of William Gaston, a member of Congress, and a Judge of the Supreme Court of North Carolina. It is bounded by the State of South Carolina and Cleveland, Lincoln, and Mecklenburg counties.[3]

---

[2] David Leroy Corbitt, *The Formation of the North Carolina Counties: 1663-1943* (Raleigh: Division of Archives and History, 1950) 147-149

[3] Ibid, 103

At one time, Mecklenburg included all North Carolina counties west of Anson and south of Rowan. It also included all or portions of the South Carolina counties of York, Chester, Lancaster, Spartanburg, Union, Cherokee, Kershaw, Laurens, Newberry and Greenville.[4] For this reason, South Carolina researchers should also consider Mecklenburg as a county to be researched.[5]

---

[4] Brent H. Holcomb and Elmer O. Parker, *Mecklenburgh County, North Carolina Deed Abstracts: 1763-1779* (South Carolina: Southern Historical Press, 1979) iii

[5] Brent H. Holcomb, *A Guide to South Carolina Genealogical Research and Records* (Privately printed, 1986) 39

Acknowledgements

The publishing of this book would not have been possible without the valuable help and assistance of the staff of the North Carolina State Archives. Their patience is legendary, and their courteous service is appreciated more than they can imagine.

Chapter One

Mecklenburg County

Civil Actions

Archibald Davie Vs. William Massey [1782]
Civil Action
Mecklenburg

Archibald Davie Vs. William Massey
Entd. in Office 7th Feby. 1787, H Milling
E:H: Bay
Levy Damgs: & Cost, £18.6.3, Not subject to the Installment Law

Camden

The State Vs a Negro Man

Mr. William Massey
You are hereby served with a Copy of this Writ of Habeas Corpus to the Intent that you may immediately appear on the Return thereof before the Honbl. Aedanus Burke Esquire to Shew Cause if any you have Why the within named Negro Man Peter should not be Left at Liberty
E.H. Bay Atty

South Carolina
To Hugh Melling Esquire Sheriff of Camden District or to any of his lawful Deputies in Said District, Greeting
You are hereby commanded that you have the Body of Peter a negro man detained in the Custody of one William Massey as it is said by whatsoever name he is called in the same, together with the day and the

Cause of the taking and detaining the said Peter before the Justice of the State aforesaid at their Chambers in Camden aforesaid immediately after the Receipt of this Writ to do and receive what the Said Justices shall then and there consider of him in his behalf. And have you then and there this Writ.

Witness the Honorable Aedanus Burke Esquire one of the aforesaid Justices of the State aforesaid at Camden this twenty ninth day of April in the Year of our Lord one thousand seven Hundred and eighty Six, And in the Tenth Year of American Independence.
E.H. Bay Attorney
Aedanus Burke

South Carolina

The State of South Carolina, To all and singular the Sheriffs of the said State, Greeting: You and each of you are hereby commanded without Delay, that of the Goods and Chattels, Houses, Lands, and other Hereditaments, and real Estates of William Massey Eighteen pounds six shillings and three pence Sterling which Archibald Davie Guardian of a certain free Negro called Peter in the Court of Common Pleas, before the Justices of the said Court at Camden lately recovered against the said William for his Damages sustained for the unlawful detaining and imprisoning the said Negro Peter as for his Costs and Charges by him expended in and about prosecuting his Suit in that Behalf, whereof the said William Stands convicted, as appears on Record:

And that you have the Money before the said justices at the said Court of Common Pleas, to be holden at Charleston, on the **[Blank]** Tuesday in **[Blank]** next, to render to the said Archibald for his Damages, Costs and Charges aforesaid. And have you then and there this Writ. Witness the Honorable John F. Grimke Esquire one of the Associate Justices at Charleston, the **[Blank]** Day of **[Blank]** in the Year of our Lord One Thousand Seven Hundred and Eighty Seven, and in the Eleventh Year of the Sovereignty and Independence of the United States of America.

E:H: Bay Plff's Atty.
J:F: Grimke Esq., £30.0.0

Recd. July 24th of **[Faded]** the Sum of Thirty pounds which **[Faded]** seven pounds **[Faded]** the whole Debt capt and **[Faded]**
William Massey

****

Susan L. Johnson Vs. Jonas W. Derr [1876]
Civil Action
Mecklenburg County

Superior Court of Mecklenburg County
Susan L. Johnston against Jonas W. Derr
Complaint

The plaintiff above named alleges For a first Cause of Action. That the Defendant on 18th Jany. 1863 Executed and delivered to her the following not Viz, $325.00 Twelve months after date I promise to pay Susan L. Johnston the sum of three Hundred twenty-five for hire of boys Jeff & Jo. I also agree to furnish the usual amount of clothing.
January 8th 1863 signed Jonas W. Derr (Seal).

I. For a second cause of action Plaintiff alleges that during the years 1864 and 1865 the said negroes Jeff & Joe continued in the Service and occupation of the said defendant, and said defendant undertook and agreed to pay the plaintiff for her said slaves what they were reasonably worth.

II. That said slaves were worth the sum of Three Hundred and Twenty five Dollars for the year 1864 and One Hundred Dollars for 1865.

III. That the defendant has paid some part of sums due plaintiff for hire of said Slaves the Exact amount of which plaintiff does not remember, Wherefore plaintiff demands Judgment against the defendant for the sum Seven Hundred and fifty Dollars and on Three Hundred and Twenty five Dollars for January 8th 1864 and interest on like amount for Jany 8th 1865 and on residue from May 1865 & cash of action.
Jones & Johnston for Pltffs

Mecklenburg County }
North Carolina }

Susan L. Johnston - Plaintiff
against
Jonas W. Derr- Defendant

This Action having been referred to me by order dated the **[Blank]** day of May 1876 to hear and decide all issues therein I respectfully report That on the 22nd day of August 1876 the same was duly brought to trial before me at my office in the City of Charlotte, Counsel for both parties attending and evidence received and thereupon I find as follows:

That this action was not brought within the time fixed by law for commencing the same and is barred by the statute of Limitations. I therefore direct Judgment to be entered against the Plaintiff for the costs of the action to be taxed by the Clerk
C.E. Grier, Referee

S. L. Johnston }
Vs.
Jonas Derr }

At a Superior Court held at the Court House in Charlotte in the County of Mecklenburg on the 20th day of Nov. 1876

Present Hon.. David Schenk Judge Ninth District
This Cause having been referred to C.E. Grier and report filed and no exceptions filed to said report. It is now on motion of W.W. Flemming Counsel for defendant adjudged that the Defendant go without day, and that he be allowed his reasonable Costs and damages to be taxed by the Clerk.
It is further ordered that the referee be allowed five dollars to be taxed with the costs.

In the Superior Court

1st The Defendant answering the Plaintiffs complaint admits that he did give the Note mentioned in allegation and that he continued to keep the Boys untill they were emancipated in 1865, and if he gave a Note or made any contract about their services after 1863 the Defendant does not recollect it. The Dollars mentioned in the complaint were of Confederate value an **[Rest of paragraph faded.]**

2nd That he has paid Plaintiff in full for the services of said Boys during the whole time for which he hired them that in the confusion of the War and about the time of the surrender many of his memorandums letters and accounts were lost or mislaid since this suit was brought looking through his old memoranda he finds items Charged to Plaintiff amounting in aggregate to $1405 of which $900 was paid to Plaintiff for James F. Johnson and that he has paid Plaintiff sums of money the precise amount he does not recollect for which his memorandums are lost.

3rd In further answer to this Complaint that Nancy Johnson & James F. Johnson have instituted similar suits against this defendant for claims due them respectively and so the young Gentlemen were absent in the War most of the time and as the Ladies lived together their articles and necessaries and money as they called for them were to be credited on general account they having authority to receive and credit the same for the services of the negroes the amounts aforesaid paid to Susan Johnson and Nancy Johnson was paid in this way and the Notes outstanding could not be produced when he called for them.

4th That in further defense of this action this suit was not brought within the time fixed by Law for bringing the same.
H.W. Guion, Atty.

****

Nancy Johnson Vs. Jonas Derr [1876
Civil Action
Mecklenburg County

North Carolina } Superior Court

Mecklenburg County }

Nancy Johnson Plaintiff
Vs.
Jonas Derr Defendant

This Action having been referred to me by order dated the [Blank] day of May 1876 to hear and decide the issues therein I respectfully report, That on the 22nd day of August 1876 the same was brought to a trial before me, at my office in Charlotte, counsel for both parties attending and evidence received, and thereupon I find as follows:

That this action was not commenced within the time prescribed by law for bringing such actions and is barred by the statutes of Limitations. I therefore direct judgment to be entered against the plaintiff for the costs of the action to be taxed by the Clerk.
C.E. Grier, Referee

Superior Court -- Mecklenburg County

Nancy Johnston
Vs.
Jonas W. Derr

Plaintiff complaining alleges in a just cause of action.

I. That on 8th January 1863 defendant executed and delivered to her the following not $200 -- twelve months after date I promise to pay Mrs. Nancy Johnston the sum of two Hundred Dollars for the hire of boy Tom. I also agree to furnish the usual amount of clothing.
January 8th 1863
Signed - Jonas W. Derr (Seal)

For a second cause of action plaintiff alleges

II. That said defendant continued to comply and had the services of the said Slave Tom for the years 1864 and 1865 said that he undertook to pay her for said Slave what he was reasonably worth for said last two years.

III. That defendant has furnished plaintiff with some provisions and has made some payment on said debts the amount of which plaintiff does not know. Wherefore plaintiff demands Judgment against defendant for the sum of Four Hundred Dollars from 8 Jany and on Two Hundred Dollars for 8 Jany 1865 and on balance for May 1865 & for costs of action
Jones Johnston

Mecklenburg County
In the Superior Court

Nancy Johnson
Vs.
Jonas W. Derr

1st The defendant answering the Plaintiffs complaints admits that he did give the Note mentioned in allegations 1st and that he continued to keep the Boy untill he was emancipated in 1865, and if he gave a Note or made any contract about about his services after 1863 the Defendant does not recollect, the Dollars mentioned in the complaint were of Confederate value and should be scaled to the value in federal currency.

2nd That he has paid the Plaintiff in full for the services of said Boy during the whole time for which he hired him that in the confusion of the War and about the time of the surrender many of his memorandums letters & accounts were lost or mislaid since this suit was brought looking through hid old memorandums he finds Items charged to her for articles furnished to **[?]** such as Lard, leather, wood and other necessaries amounting in the agregate to $2536.77

3rd In further answer to this complaint that Susan Johnson & James F. Johnson have instituted similar Suits against this Defendant for them respectively and as the young Gentlemen were absent in the War most of the time and as the Ladies **[?]** together articles and necessaries and money as they called for them were to be credited on General account they having authority to receive and credit the same for the services of the negroes the amount aforesaid paid to Nancy Johnson was paid in this way and the Notes outstanding could not be produced when he called for them.

4th That in addition to the payments aforesaid the Girl Mariah was sent with two Children to this defendant to take care of without any contract on his part she was no service to him & being in a breeding condition she had two more Children during the War and he did take care of them as an accomodation to the family and that he should be paid for the same.

5th That this suit was not brought within the time proved by Law
H. W. Guion, Atty.

Nancy Johnston
Vs.
Jonas Derr
At a Superior Court held at the Court House in Charlotte in the County of Mecklenburg on the 20th day of Nov. 1876

Present Hon. David Schenck Judge Ninth District
This cause having been referred to C.E. Grier and report filed and no exceptions filed to said report. It is now on motion of W.W. Fleming Counsel for Defendant adjudged that the Defendant go without day, and that he be allowed his reasonable costs and damages to be taxed by the Clerk.

It is further ordered that the referee be allowed five dollars to be taxed with the Costs.
D. Schenck, Judge - 9th Dist.

****

James F. Johnson Vs. Jonas W. Derr [1876]
Civil Action
Mecklenburg County

Superior Court -- Mecklenburg County

James F. Johnson
Vs.
Jonas W. Derr

Plaintiff complaining alleges for a Just Cause of Action

That on 8 January 1863 the defendant executed and delivered to him the **note of which the following is a true copy $400 -- Twelve months after** date I promise to pay James F. Johnston Four Hundred Dollars for the hire [**?**] Tina[**?**] & Hose[**?**] -- I also agree to provide said negroes with the usual amount of clothing Jany 8, 1863
Signs Jonas W. Derr (Seal)

For a second cause of action plaintiff alleges that defendant had the services of the Slaves Tina[**?**] & Besey[**Berry?**] for the year 1864 and 1865 and undertook to pay what same were reasonably worth
That they were worth per year Four Hundred Dollars
That Defendant paid to the Plaintiff on account of said debts

Wherefore plaintiff demand Judgment for Twelve Hundred Dollars & interest on Four Hundred Dollars for Jany 1864 and on interest on like amount for Jany 8, 1865 and on like amt. from Jany 8, 1866
Jones ---- Johnston, for Plff

Mecklenburg County

1st The Defendant answering the Plaintiffs complaint admits that he did give the Note mentioned in allegation No. 1. He does not recollect whether or not he employed the Negroes after 1863 but if he did the services were less valuable every year after that, And the Dollars mentioned are Confederate Dollars and are subject to the Confederate scale.

2nd That he has paid the Plaintiff in full for the Services of said Boys during the whole time for which he hired them that in the confusion of the War and about the time of the surrender many of his memorandums letters and accounts were lost or mislaid. Since this suit was brought looking through his old memoranda he finds Items charged to Nancy Johnson for the use and benefit of the family such artickles as Lard, flour, wood and other necessaries amounting in aggregate of $1405 of which was paid to her $900 for plaintiff.

3rd In further answer to this complaint that Nancy Johnson and Susan Johnson have instituted Similar suits against this Defendant for claims due them respectively as the Plaintiff and the other young Gentleman were most of the time in the War and as the Ladies lived together such articles and necessaries and many as they called for them were furnished to be Credited on General account they having authority to receive and credit the same for the services of the negroes the amount aforesaid paid to them was paid in this way and the Notes outstanding could not be produced when he called for them.

4th That this suit was not brought within the time fixed by Law.

Jonas Derr, Defendant in the above Intitled action being sworn says that the facts contained in the affidavit in the cause of James F. Johnston and Jonas Derr are **[Rest of sentence faded]**
J.W. Derr
Sworn to & subscribed before me 6th March 1876
J.R. Erwin C.S.C.
By S J Thompson D.C.

[The text in this document is faded in many areas.]

In the Superior Court
James F. Johnston
Vs.
Jonas Derr

Jonas Derr the Defendant in this Cause being sworn says that he cannot as he is **[?]** and believes have a fair and impartial trial of this cause in Mecklenburg County, That the Defendants **[Plaintiffs]** are of a large and influential family and that this together with the fact that as he has been **[?]** believes the regular price of negro hire was to be established by

Common Consent and by continued introduction of Witness who have settled or what they think to be a fair valuation [?] from what they were worth at the time but from what a mans labor would reasonably be worth now and That he is [?] and believes That in [?] for the hire of negroes during the War a fair and impartial trial Can not be had in this Cause [?] that this affidavit is not [?] delay but to insure Justice.
J.W. Derr
Sworn to & Subscribed before me 6th day of March 1876
John R. Erwin C.S.C.
By S J Thompson D.C.

North Carolina } Superior Court
Mecklenburg County }

James F. Johnston, Plaintiff
Vs.
Jonas W. Derr, Defendant

This action having been referred to me by order dated May 1876 to hear and decide the issues I respectfully report.

That on the 22nd day of August 1876 the same was brought to trial before me at my office at Charlotte Counsel for both sides being present and evidence received and thereupon I find as follows.

That this action was not instituted within the time presented by Law for commencing such action and is barred by the Statute of Limitations, I therefore direct -- Judgment to be entered against the plaintiff for the cost of the Action to be taxed by the Clerk.
C.E. Grier Referee

Received of Jonas Derr two dollars in part payment of my attendance in Case of James F. Johnston Vs Jonas Derr which I direct to be paid out of my witness ticket in said Case.

his
Test C.E. Grier Hosea X Johnston
mark

At a Superior Court held at the Court House in Charlotte, in the County of Mecklenburg on the 20th day of Nov. 1876.

J. F. Johnston
Vs.
Jonas Derr

Present Hon. David Schenck Judge Ninth District

This cause having been referred to C.E. Grier and report filed, and no exceptions filed to said report, It is now on motion of W. W. Flemming Counsel for Defendant adjudged that the Defendant go without day and that he be allowed his reasonable costs and damages to be taxed by the Clerk.

It is further ordered that the referee be allowed five dollars to be taxed with the costs.

D. Schenck, Judge, 9th Dist.

****

Sophronia West & Others Vs. Edward Sloan [1855]
Civil Action
Mecklenburg County

Lincolnton, Feb. 24th 1855

Dear Sir,

Enclosed you will an original bill in Equity, with a pross bond and an affidavit as to absent defendant. You will **[Torn]** forth with issue **[Torn]** act of assembly as to the absent defendant and much oblige your **[?]** Quinn & Lander

Dr. Dunlap, Charlotte

Pross. Bond signed by W. Slade & E.S. Barrott for $200

Court of Equity }
Mecklenburg County } SS.

The State of North Caroina
To Sarah N. Sloan Greeting:

For certain reasons offered before the Honourable Court of Equity for the County aforesaid, you the said Sarah N. Sloan are commanded and strictly enjoined, that, laying all other matters aside, and notwithstanding any excuse, you personally appear before the said Court, To be held at the Court House in Charlotte on the 7th Monday after the 4th Monday in March next, then and there to answer concerning those things which shall then and there be objected to you by Fanny West & others, and to do further, and to receive what the said Court shall consider in this behalf; and this you shall in no wise omit, under the penalty of one hundred pounds.

Witness, David R. Dunlap Clerk and Master in our said Court, at Office, and under the Seal of Office, the 7th after the 4th Monday in Sept. 1854. Issued the 21st day of March 1855.
D.R. Dunlap C.M.E.

Court of Equity }
Mecklenburg County } SS.

The State of North Carolina,
To William M. Stinson & wife Ellin Greeting:

For certain reasons offered before the Honorable Court of Equity for the County aforesaid, you the said William M. Stinson are commanded and strictly enjoined, that, laying all other matters aside, and notwithstanding any excuse, you personally appear before the said Court, to be held at the Court House in Charlotte on the 7th Monday after the 4th Monday in March next, then and there to answer concerning those things which shall then and there be objected to you by Fanny West & Others, and do further, and to receive what the said Court shall consider in this behalf; and this you shall in no wise omit, under the penalty of one hundred pounds.

Witness David R. Dunlap Clerk and Master in our said Court, at Office, and under the Seal of office, the 7th Monday after the 4th Monday in Septr. 1854. Issued the 21st day of March 1855.
D.R. Dunlap C.M.C.

Court of Equity }
Mecklenburg County } SS.

The State of North Carolina,
To David Sloan, Greeting:

For certain reasons offered before the Honorable Court of Equity for the County aforesaid, you the said David Sloan are commanded and strictly enjoined, that, laying all other matters aside, and notwithstanding any excuse, you personally appear before the said Court to be held at the Court House in Charlotte on the 7th Monday after the 4th Monday in March next, then and there to answer concerning those things which shall then and there be objected to you by Fanny West & others, and to do further, and to receive what the said Court shall consider in this behalf; and this you shall in no wise omit, under the penalty of one hundred pounds.

Witness David R. Dunlap, Clerk and Master in our said Court, at Office, and under the Seal of office, the 7th Monday after the 4th Monday in Septr. 1854. Issued the 21st day of March 1855.
D.R. Dunlap C.M.E.

Court of Equity }
Mecklenburg County } SS.

The State of North Carolina,
To Samuel Johnson & wife Lucinda Greeting:

For certain reasons offered before the Honorable Court of Equity for the County aforesaid, you the said Samuel Johnson are commanded and strictly enjoined, that, laying all other matters aside, and notwithstanding any excuse, you personally appear before the said Court, to be held at the Court House in Charlotte on the 7th Monday after the 4th Monday in March next, then and there to answer concerning those things which shall then and there be objected to you by Fanny West & others, and to do further, and to receive what the said Court shall consider in this behalf; and this you shall in no wise omit, under the penalty of one hundred pounds.

Witness, David R. Dunlap, Clerk and Master in our said Court, at Office, and under Seal of office, the 7th Monday after the 4th Monday in Septr. 1854. Issued the 21st day of March 1855.
D.R. Dunlap C.M.E.

Court of Equity }
Mecklenburg County } SS.

The State of North Carolina
To E.B.D. Sloan & wife Rebecca Greeting:

For certain reasons offered before the Honorable Court of Equity for the County aforesaid, you the said E.B.D. Sloan are commanded and strictly enjoined, that, laying all other matters aside, and notwithstanding any excuse, you personally appear before the said Court to be held at the Court House in Charlotte on the 7th Monday after the 4th Monday in March next, then and there to answer concerning those things which shall then and there be objected to you by Fanny West, William C. West, Columbus D. West & others, and to do further, and to receive what the said Court shall consider in this behalf; and this you shall in no wise omit, under the penalty of one hundred pounds.

Witness, David R. Dunlap, Clerk and Master in our said Court, at Office, and under Seal of office, the 7th Monday after the 4th Monday in Septr. 1854. Issued the 20th day of March 1855.
D.R. Dunlap, C.M.E.

Court of Equity }
Mecklenburg County } SS.

The State of North Carolina,
To A.A. Kennady & wife Jane Greeting:

For certain reasons offered before the Honorable Court of Equity for the County aforesaid, you the said A.A. Kennady are commanded and strictly enjoined, that, laying all other matters aside, and notwithstanding any excuse, you personally appear before the said Court to be held at the Court House in Charlotte on the 7th Monday after the 4th Monday in March next, then and there to answer concerning those things which shall then and there be objected to you by Fanny West & others, and to do further, and to receive what the said Court shall consider in this behalf; and this you shall in no wise omit, under the penalty of one hundred pounds.

Witness, David R. Dunlap, Clerk and Master in oyr said Court, at Office, and under Seal of office, the 7th Monday after the 4th Monday in Septr. 1854. Issued 21st day of March 1855.
D.R. Dunlap C.M.E.

Haywood W. Guin
Attorney for Elvira West & others

The deposition of John Sloan will be taken at his residence in the town of Charlotte on Tuesday the 8th day of August to be read as Evidence in the suit pending in Mecklenburg Court of Equity wherein Elvira West & others are plaintiffs and Edward B.D. Sloan & others are defendants.
James W. Osborne, Atto. for deft.

A copy of the Within delivered to W. Lander Esqr.
27th of October 1855
C. Milten, Shff

Came to hand the 27th day of October 1855
C. Milten, Shff

Wm. Lander Esqr.

The deposition of John Sloan will be taken at his residence in the Town of Charlotte on Saturday the 3d day of October next to be read as evidence in the Case of Sophronia West and others vs. Edwd. Sloan & others, Oct 25, 1835
Mecklenburg Court of Equity
James W. Osborne, Sol.

North Carolina
Supreme Court December Term 1856
Fanny West & others agt. E.B.D. Sloan & others

This Cause coming on to be heard in the bill answers proofs & exhibits & being debated by the Counsel for the plaintiffs & the defendants, it is considered & declared to be the opinion of the Court that James Sloan the Trustee appointed under the Will of Sarah Sloan did not make a bonafide sale of the Slave Hannah & her Children to William A. Stinson, but that the transaction Set up by the Defendants as such was fraudulent & void & that the said James Sloan continued to hold the said property as the trustee of the said Fanny West & her children till his death -- that there never has been a settlement & closing of the trust aforesaid, and no such **[?]** or acquiescence of the plaintiff as to bar their rights of recovery. It is further declared to be the opinion of the Court that Benjamin F. West, the husband of Fanny could **[Torn]** have been a formal party if he were alive, but he is now dead. It is further declared to be the opinion of the Court that A.C. Miller purchased Elvira & her two children fairly & without notice of the plaintiffs equity & that E.B.D. Sloan & Samuel Johnston who hold the remainder of the said Slave **[Torn]** volunteers having paid nothing for them. It is therefore ordered & adjudged & decreed that Walter P. Caldwell Esquire be appointed a commissioner to enquire concerning the descendants of the slave Hannah in the hands of the defendants & that he state an account of the values of the Services of said slaves in the hands of E.B.D. Sloan & Samuel Johnston. He will also enquire as to the fund for which Elvira & her children were sold to A.C. Miller. He will also state an account of the administration of the said trusts by James Sloan allowing for all payments made by him to Mrs. West & he will report to the next term of this Court. In taking the account as to the values of the hires of the slaves the Commissioner will allow the defendants credits for the expense of raising & keeping unprofitable slaves -- It is further ordered, adjudged & decreed that Haywood W. Guin Esquire be appointed trustee of Mrs. Fanny West & her children & that the defendants E.B.D. Sloan & Samuel Johnson deliver the slaves held by them to said trustee at such time, place as he may require. Ordered further that the defendants except A.C. Miller pay the costs of this suit to be charged by the Clerk.
A true Copy
E.B. Freeman, Clerk

North Carolina }In Equity

Mecklenburg County }

To the Sheriff of Mecklenburg County, greeting:

You are hereby commanded to Summon T.N. Alexander, H.B. Williams, Wm. Ross, Geo. Cross & Saml. A. Harris, Cap. Slade, Saml. Frisby, John S. Means to be & appear at the Office of the Clerk & Master in Equity, in the Court House in Charlotte on Wednesday the 13th Inst. to testify in a Case on trial wherein Fanny West & others are complainants & E.B.D. Sloan & others are Defendants. Herein fail not.

Witness D.R. Dunlap Clerk & Master in Equity this 12th of May 1857.

D.R. Dunlap C.M.E.

Mecklenburg
North Carolina
Supreme Court - June Term 1858
Fanny West & others agt. E.B.D. Sloan & others.

This cause coming on for further directions upon the report of Mr. Commissioner Caldwell as amended & reformed, it is ordered & decreed that the same be in all things confirmed - and it is further ordered & decreed that the plaintiffs have & recover from E.B.D. Sloan the sum of thirteen hundred & fifty six dollars fifty cents ($1356.50) with interest thereon from the first day of July 1857 until paid & that they recover from Samuel Johnson thirteen hundred & fifty dollars ($1350) with interest thereon from the 1st day of July 1857 until paid. It is ordered & decreed with the consent of Counsel that Mr. Caldwell be allowed for taking the accounts one hundred dollars - thirty seven & a half dollars ($37.50) of which is to be Paid by the plaintiffs & the remainder by the defendants Sloan & Johnston.

A true copy
E.B. Freeman Clk.

****

Isaac & John M. Wilson Vs. John W. Means [1835]
Civil Action
Mecklenburg County

No. Carolina }
Mecklenburgh County } In Equity

To the Honourable the Judge of the Court of Equity of Mecklenburgh County. The Bill of Complaint of John & Isaac Wilson of Said County Humbly complaining your Orator Show unto your Honor that John M. Wilson departed this **[Life]** in the year 1831 having first made & duly published a last Will & Testament which hath been duly proved in the County Court of said County, that in & by said Will he appointed your Orators & their Brother Alexander Wilson Executors, that your Orators alone qualified & took upon themselves the execution of said Trust, the said Alexander declined & hath not taken any part in the business of Said estate. That Said Testator left him surviving among other children, a daughter Margaret who had in the life time of the Said Testator intermarried with one John Williams of Cabarrus Co. Further complaining your Orators sheweth that said last Will & Teatament among others contains the following clauses to wit "In favor of my daughter Margaret I will & bequeath that all the property of John Means purchased by me at the various Sales of his property of whatever kind whether real or personal the Speir or Burns place excepted, be vested in the hands of her Brothers towit, Alexr., Isaac & John as Trustees to be managed for her use & benefit & that of her family & finally that the whole property descend to her children according to her will & pleasure. I further Will & bequeath that should I gain the the negro girl Margaret now at issue in Law that she descend to her according to the same rules & regulations. Also my Negro Boy Alexr. now in her possession," all which will more fully appear by reference to said will a copy of which they are ready to produce when required by this Honorable Court. Further complaining your Orators sheweth that they with the said Alexander Wilson are the Brothers of said Margaret, & that said Alexr. hath wholly refused to act as trustee under the said Will & hath not in any way intermeddled therewith or with the property. Further complaining your Orators sheweth that said Means in the lifetime the Testator became greatly embarrassed, insomuch that his property was on several occasions sold under executions against him, that their Testator among other property of said Means purchased at the Executions sales aforesaid negroes Jack, Zipp or Zippa, Laura & Ann, that said Ann since the death of their Testator hath had a child named **[Blank]** that said negroes with the negro Alexr. hath remained with the said

Means since the death of their Testator for the use & benefit of said Margaret & family. Further complaining your Orators sheweth, that said Means is as they believe entirely insolvent, that he has threatened to sell said Negroes on some occasions & in others has threatened to remove them beyond the limits of this State & they fear that he will Carry said threats into execution. Said Slaves are worth at this time as they believe the sum of three thousand dollars. your Orators are alarmed that should said Means sell or remove said Negroes so as to prevent them from executions said trust that they would become individually responsible & that they have no way to prevent such a catastrophy but by the interposition of this Honourable Court. In tender consideration of all which & forasmuch as your Orators are without remedy save only in this Honorable Court where matters of this kind are properly cognizable & relievable. to the end therefore that the said Jno Means may upon his Corporal Oath true answer make to all & Singular the facts herein Set forth as fully as tho' the same were depicted & he thereto specially interrogated & that your Honor would grant unto your Orators your Writ of Ne Esceat & such other setup as shall seem agreeably to Equity & good conscience. And May it please your Honor to grant unto your Orators your States Writ of Subpoena directed to the Sheriff of Cabarrus Commanding him to summon the said Jno Means to appear at the next Court of Equity to be held for said County of Mecklenburg to answer the promiser[?] & abide the decree of the Court.
D.L. Caldwell, Solr.

N. Carolina

Complainents maketh oath that the several matters & things set forth in the foregoing Bill which are of their own knowledge are true & those not of their own knowledge they believe to be true.
Isaac Wilson & J.M. Wilson

Sworn to & subscribed before us this 14th day of Decr. 1835.
D.R. Dunlap C.M.E.

State of North Carolina

The Clerk and Master of the County of Mecklenburg, is ordered, on the Complainants giving bond and security as required by law, to issue an Injunction to John Means of the County of Cabarrus, commanding and

enjoining him not to sell or remove, or cause to be removed, the negro Slaves Jack, Zipp or Zippa, Ann or her child, mentioned in this Bill as bequeathed to the Complainants, John and Isaac Wilson, in trust, by John M. Wilson deceased; or any other of the property or effects so bequeathed in trust to the Co,plainants by the said Testator; and that he do not in any other way or manner hinder, obstruct, or delay the Complainants in the legal and proper execution of the trusts confided to them by the said Testator in and his last Will and Testament - 24th Decr. 1835.
Wm. Norwood JSCSE

State of North Carolina } In Equity
Mecklenburgh County }

To The Honourable the Judge, now, setting in Chancery for the County aforesaid.

The answer of John W. Means Defendant to the Bill of Complaint of John and Isaac Wilson Complainants.

This Defendant Saving and reserving [?] answer to said bill or to so much thereof, as he is advised it is material for him to make answer unto, answering, saith he admits it is true as alledged in Complainants Bill that John M. Wilson departed this life, having first duly published his last will and testament -- That said will contains the bequest as set forth in the bill - that Complainants are Trustees as in said bill charged - This Defendant for further answer does most positively deny that he has any intention of removing the said Negroes beyond the limits of the State - and he does in the same positive manner deny that he has any intention to sell said negroes - That negro traders have frequently offered to purchase at large prices - and that he has uniformly refused to sell - This Defendant denies that he has threatened to sell said negroes - This Defendant for further answer states that some time in July 1835 the Complainants while said negroes were in Defendants possession sold them to one Milton Morrison for less than what he believed to be their value - That after the sale they attempted to take said negroes from your Defendants possession by force - that when they failed thus to obtain possession the possession of said negroes - an action of Detinue was commenced to recover them - and while said action was pending - the strange proceeding of the writ of repletion [?] under our act of Assembly was [?] out against your

Defendant although said slaves had been in the continual possession of your defendant for about Eighteen years. Your Defendant states that while this extraordinary Cause was pursued against him, he enquired he had not a right to sell - as he was offered a much larger price for said negroes than what the Trustees sold for - Your Defendant states that if he had been advised that he could have sold - it was not with the intention of defeating the bointy of the Testator but to increase the fund - Your Defendant must believe that when the Trustees sold they were consulting more with their private interests - than the interest of your Defendant, his wife and seven children, as they were residing on a farm - and it would have been almost impossible for them to get on without the services of said slaves - Your Defendant for further answer states that the Trustees on one occasion were desirous to sell the Lands on which he resides - that your Defendant objected to the sale - and then Complainants were anxious for your Defendant to take the negroes and remove to Tennessee - your Defendant having answered all the material allegations of the bill pray to be dismissed with his costs.
Jno. Giles, Sol. for Defendant

State of North Carolina
Mecklenburg County

This day personally appeared before me the Defendant John W. Means and made oath that the several matters of facts and things set forth in this his answer which are of his own knowledge are true - and those stated not of his own knowledge he believes to be true.
Sworn to & Subscribed before me Feby. 23rd 1836
J.W. Means
Sworn to & Subscribed before me Feby. 23rd 1836
D.R. Dunlap C.M.E.

Isaac & John Wilson Trustees } In Equity
Vs
Jno W. Means }

This Cause coming on to be heard upon the Bill answers & [?] & the motion of the defendant to [?] the Ne Esceat & Injunction & the parties being heard by Counsel & the matter considered by the Court it is ordered & declared that the motion to dissolve is refused and upon motion of complainants counsel it is ordered & declared that the said Ne Esceat & Injunction be perpetuated and that the bond Esceated by defendant & others for the forth coming of the Negroes in complainants Bill set forth, be held by the Master of this Court for the benefit of complainants & subject to the further order of this Court, and it is further ordered that the question of **[?]** be **[?]**.

John & Isaac Wilson } August Term 1838
Vs
John Means }

This Cause coming in for final decree touching the cost incurred it is ordered that Complainants pay one half of the cost & defendant pay the other half - No Tax fees to be taxed on either side.

Isaac & John M. Wilson
Vs
John W. Means
Subpo.

In February Term 1836
The defedt. John W. Means Summoned according to Subpoena & copy **[?]** plainants.
Delivered January 30th 1836
W.H. Archibald Shff

Court of Equity }
Mecklenburg County } Court of Equity - Aug. Sess.

The State of North Carolina,
To John W. Means of Cabarrus County, Greeting:

For certain reasons offered before the Honorable Court of Equity for the County aforesaid, you the said John W. Means are commanded and strictly enjoined, that, laying all other matters aside, and notwithstanding any excuse, you personally appear before the said Court, to be held at the

Court House in Charlotte on the 3rd Monday in February next, then and there to answer concerning those things which shall then and there be objected to you by Isaac Wilson & John M. Wilson, Trustees of Margaret Means, and to do further, and to receive what the said Court shall consider in this behalf; and this you shall in no wise omit, under the penalty of one hundred pounds.

Witness, David R. Dunlap Clerk and Master in our said Court, at Office, and under Seal of office, the last Monday of August 1835. Issued the 4th day of Jany. 1836.
D.R. Dunlap C.M.E.

Isaac & John M. Wilson
Vs
John W. Means of Cabarrus

To February Term 1836
D.F. Caldwell

Issued 1 copy 7 & 2/8 Cop Shts.	1.54
Injunct. & Ne Esceat	1.00
Subpa.	1.00
Bond	.30

4th Jany. 1836

Doct. David Dunlap, Charlotte, No. Car.

North Carolina }
Mecklenburg County } To the Sheriff of Cabarrus County, Greeting

Whereas complaint has been made to our Honourable Court of Equity, by Isaac & John M. Wilson, Trustees of Margaret Means, wife of John W. Means, That sd. J.W. Means has now in his possession certain negroes Viz. Alexr, Jack, Zepp or Zippa, Ann & her child & other property which was bequeathed to sd. Isaac & John M. by their late father the Revd. John M. Wilson, in trust for the use & benefit of their Sister Margaret Means & her children - And which negroes & property sd. Means threatens to remove beyond the limits of this State - & whereas their complaint has been heard and an Order made that a Writ of Injunction or Ne Exeat issue, expressly injoining and forbidding such removal - And whereas the sd. Isaac & John Trustees as aforesaid have given their bond & security as the Law, in such Cases requires.

You are therefore commanded to take into your possession the sd. negroes, Alexr., Jack, Zipp or Zippa, Laura & Ann & her child and them safely keep to abide the Order of this Honourable Court unless the sd. **John W. Means shall enter into bond with good & sufficient security in** the sum of Six thousand Dollars, conditioned that he neither sell or remove sd. negroes or any other property so bequeathed, but Surrender thenm when demanded by Order of this Court. And have you this Writ at our next Court House in Charlotte on the 3rd Monday of February next, there to show how or in what manner you have executed the same. Herein fail not.

Witness David R. Dunlap Clerk & Master in Equity, at Office, in Charlotte, the last Monday in Augst. AD 1835 & in the 60th year of American Independence. issued 4th day of Jany. 1836.
D.R. Dunlap C.M.E.

No. Carolina }
Mecklenburg County }

Know all whom it may concern that we Isaac Wilson, John M. Wilson & Stephen Fox acknowledge ourselves indebted to John W. Means in the penal sum of six thousand dollars, to the which payment well & truly to be made, We bind ourselves our heirs Exrs. & Amrs. jointly & severally by these presents - Witness our hands & seals this **[Blank]** day of **[Blank]** 1836.

The Condition of the above obligation is such that whereas the above mentioned Isaac & John Wilson, as Trustees for their Sister Margaret Means, have this day filed a bill in Equity against the sd. John W. Means, and therein prayed out a Writ of Injunction & Ne Esceat expressly forbidding sd. Means to remove beyond the Limits of this State, certain negroes & other property of the value of three thousand Dollars, now in his posssession which was beqieathed by the late Revd. John M. Wilson in his last Will & Testament, to the sd. Isaac & John M. Wilson in Trust for the use & benefit of the said Margaret Means, wife of John W.

Means, & her children - And whereas sd. Prayer of Petitioner has been heard and a Writ of Ne Esceat ordered to be issued, and also a Writ of Subpoena Commanding sd. Means to be & appear at the next Court of Equity to answer sd. Bill of Complaint. Now if the sd. Isaac & John, Trustees as aforesaid shall succeed in this cause, or if they fail therein shall well & truly pay all such costs and Charges as may or shall be decreed against them, then this obligation to be void or otherwise to remain in full force and Virtue - Witness our hands & seals the day & year above written

J.M. Wilson (Seal)
St. Fox (Seal)

No. Carolina

Know all men by these presents we the undersigned are held & firmly bound unto Isaac & Jno M. Wilson in the penal sum of six thousand dollars to which payment we bind ourselves & our heirs.

Whereas heretofore the above named Isaac & Jno. M. Wilson as Trustees of Margaret Means filed their Bill in the Court of Equity of Mecklenburgh County against Jno W. means Instant of said Margaret praying among other things that the said Jno. W. be Injoined from selling, removing or otherwise disposing of certain Negroes by them held as trustees under the Will of their deceased Father towit Alexr., Zipp or Zippa, Laura & Ann & her child. And whereas the Judge of said Court hath ordered that said Negroes be taken & safely kept by the Sheriff of Cabarrus, unless the said Jno W. enter into Bond conditional as in said order mentioned.

The condition of the above obligation therefore is such, that if the said Jon Williams neither sell or remove said Negroes from the State, And have them forthcoming to which the order of said Court then the above obligation to be void. Feby. 9th 1836

Test. Edwd. R. Gobson
J.W. Means (Seal)
P. Barringer (Seal)
Robert S. Means (Seal)
George Miller (Seal)

State of North Carolina.
To the Sheriff of Cabarrus County, Greeting:

We command you, that of the goods and chattels, lands and tenements of John W. Means, if to be found in your bailiwick, you cause to be made the sum of **[Blank]** which, in the Superior Court of Law, held for the County of Mecklenburg at the Court House in Charlotte - Isaac & John Wilson recovered against him for **[?]** and the sum of six dollars & twenty eight & half cents ($6.28 1/2) for costs and charges in the said suit expended, whereof the said John W. Means is liable, as appears to us of record. And have you the said moneys, besides your fees for this service, before the Judge of our said Court at Charlotte aforesaid, on the 3rd Monday of February next, then and there to render the said Isaac & John Wilson the costs and charges aforesaid. herein fail not; and have you then and there this writ.

Witness, David R. Dunlap Clerk of our said Court, at Office in Charlotte the 3rd Monday in August in the 64th year of our Independence, A.D. 1839.
D.R. Dunlap C.M.E.

Isaac & John Wilson
Vs
John W. Means
Fe. Fa.
To February Term 1840
To hand 12 Decr.
Costs

C. & M	10.56 ½
W.H.A. Shff of Cabarrus	2.00
	12.56 ½
Each party to pay half	6.28 ¼

Six dollars and twenty eight ¼ cents collected and two dollars paid to W.H.A. former sheriff fee as per receipt on Fe Fa balance paid to Officer in Cash.
L B Krimmings Shff

Recd. of Shff of Cabarrus my fee
WA Archibald, former Shff, 7.32 ½

****

Isaac Campbell Vs. William Alexander [1810]
Civil Action
Mecklenburg County

State of North Carolina }
Mecklenburg County } In Equity

To the Honorable the Judge of the Court of Equity for the County of Mecklenburg now sitting in Chancery, humbly Complaining sheweth to your Honor your Orator Isaac Campbell of the County aforesaid, That some time heretofore a certain William Alexander of the County aforesaid made and duly executed to your Orator a mortgage to a negro boy in the words and figures following Viz

"Know all men by these presents that I William Alexander of the State of North Carolina and County of Mecklenburg for and in Consideration of the Sum of one **[Torn]** bill of receipt whereof hereby acknowledged **[Torn]** sold and delivered and by these presents do bargain sell and deliver unto the said Isaac Campbell his Executors, Administrators or assigns forever one negroe boy named Sam to have and to hold and I do hereby bind myself, my heirs or executors to warrant and defend against all claims the said boy unto the said Isaac Campbell his heirs, executors. or assigns, Provided nevertheless that if the said William Alexander my executors, administrators or assigns or any of as do and shall well and truly pay or Cause to be paid unto the said Isaac Campbell his executors, administrators or assigns the sum of one hundred and fifty dollars on or before the first day of January next ensuing the date hereof for the redemption of the said bargained premises then the bill of sale to be void, otherwise to remain in full force & virtue. In witness whereof I have hereunto set my hand and seal this 10th day of August 1810."
Test John How Wm Alexander (Seal)

But now so it is may it please your Honor that the said William Alexander doth refuse to pay your Orator the aforesaid sum of one hundred and fifty dollars or to deliver to your Orator the negroe boy Sam mortgaged as aforesaid although often thereunto requested in a friendly manner. In tender consideration whereof and forasmuch as your Orator is remideless in the premises save in this honorable Court, to the end **[Torn]** to all and singular the premises in as simple manner as though the same one herein again repeated and he thereunto especially interrogated and that he may be compelled by a decree of this Court as your Honor may direct to surrender to your Orator the possession of the said negroe boy Sam and that the Equity of the redemption of said Mortgage may be foreclosed and so remain and that your Honor would grant to your Orator such other and further relief in the premises as to your Honor may seem meet and just and the nature of the Case may regain -- May it please your Honor to grant to your Orator a Writ of Subpoena to be directed to the said William Alexander Commanding him on a Certain day and under a certain penalty therein named to appear and answer the several matters & things herein set forth &c.
And your Orator will ever pray &c
Jo [?] Compl**[Torn]**

****

J.W. Blair Vs. E.C. Wallis & Ira Parks [1867]
Civil Action
Mecklenburg County

January 29th, 1867
$432.00

One day after date we promise to pay to the order of Jno: W. Blair Four Hundred & Thirty Two Dollars Valur received

Witness our hands & Seals

This note is for hire of	E.C. Wallis	(Seal)
boy Green before the War	Ira Parks	(Seal)

J.W. Blair }
Vs. }April 1st 1868
EC Wallis & Ira Parks }

Defendant EC Wallis maketh oath that the note upon which this [?] was brought was given for the hire of Negro during the late war & that there is no other [?] therefore - & that he desires to have benefit of late Order of [?] County.

Sworn & Subscribed this 18th day of April 1868
Wm. Maxwell CLC E.C. Wallis

Superior Court - Mecklenburg County

At a Superior Court held at the Court House in Charlotte, in the County of Mecklenburg, on the 22 day of Nov 1869.

JW Blair Against EC Wallis & Ira Parks

Present, Honorable JW Logan, Judge Ninth District.
This action having been brought to a trial by the Court, a trial by Jury having been waived, and a decision therein rendered for the Plaintiff., it is now, on motion of B,[?] Counsel for the Plaintiff.

Adjudged, That the Plaintiff recover of the Defendant Five hundred and nineteen & 14 ($519.14) dollars, of which Four Hundred thirty two dollars in pincipal Seventy two [?] dollars is interest, and Fourteen 10 dollars is costs of action, with interest on said principal until paid.

****

Whitley Vs. Pettus [1862]
Civil Action
Mecklenburg County

State of North Carolina }

Mecklenburg County }

Personally appeared before me Jennings B. Kerr Clerk of the Superior Court for said County Robert D. Whitley and made oath in due form of law that he has been ib possession of a negro boy slave named Elic - aged about 55 or 60 years dark complexion worth about three hundred dollars within two years from the date hereof, and that he has been deprived of the possession of said Slave by John F. Pettus of said County. Sworn to & subscribed before me this 16th day of August 1862.
RD Whitley
JB Kerr Clerk SC

State of North Carolina
To the Sheriff of Mecklenburg County Greeting
Whereas Robert D. Whitley has made oath that Elic a Slave aged about 55 or 60 years of dark complexion has been in his lawful possession within two years from the date hereof, and that he has been deprived of the possession of the said Slave by John F. Pettus the defendant without his consent or permission and whereas the said Robert D. Whitley hath further made oath that the said slave is of the value of three hundred dollars and hath also given bond with approved security in the sum of six hundred dollars payable to the said John F. Pettus conditional to perform the final judgement which may be rendered in this suit of [?] & hath also given bond with security for the prosecution of the Suit.

You are therefore commanded forthwith to take the said slave into your custody if to be found in your County and deliver him to the said Plaintiff, unless the said defendant shall execute & deliver to you a bond with approved security in the Sum of Six hundred dollars payable to the said plaintiff and conditional to perform the final Judgment which shall be rendered in this suit and if the aforesaid defendant shall execute & deliver to you a bond as aforesaid you are commanded to return said bond with this suit.

You are further commanded to summon the said John F. Pettus the said defendant if to be found in your County to Appear before the Honourable Judge of our Superior Court of law to be held for the County of Mecklenburg at the Court House in Charlotte on the eleventh Monday after the fourth Monday of September next then and there to answer the said Robert D. Whitley of a plea of [?] and unjustly detain the said Slave

Elic to his damage two hundred dollars when and where you shall make known how you shall have executed this suit.

Witness Jennings B. Kerr Clerk of our said Court at office the 1st Monday after the 4th Monday of September 1861. Issued Aug. 16th 1862.
J.B. Kerr CM SC

The Subscribers acknowledge themselves indebted to defendant J.F. Pettus in the sum of two hundred dollars to be void on condition pltff prosecute this suit with effect or in case of failure shall pay to defendant all such costs and arrearages as shall be awarded against him.

Witness our hands & Seals — R.D. Whitley (Seal)
Aug. 16th 1862 — Wm. P. Little (Seal)

RD Whitley Vs John F. Pettus
Replevin Writ
To Fall Term 1862

Executed by taking the Boy Elic into my Custody Aug. 22nd 1862 and confining him in jail for the want of the defendant failing to give Bond and delivering Said Boy Elic to the Plaintiff Robert D. Whitley August 26th 1862, and John F. Pettus Summoned to appear at the Fall Term of the Superior Court - Aug. 25th 1862
W.W. Grier Sheriff
To hand Thursday Evening August 21st 1862
WW Grier Shff.

****

Hodges Vs. Wallace & Others [1864]
Civil Action
Mecklenburg County

Patrick A. Hodges
Vs
James Wallace & others
To Spring Term 1864

Defendants summoned, Property not to be found in my county

Jany 5th, 1864
R.M. White Shff

State of North Carolina }
Mecklenburg County }

Personally appeared before me Jennings B. Kerr, Clerk of the Superior Court of Law for said County Patrick A. Hodges and made oath in due form of law that he hath been within the last three years in the lawfull possession of a negro girl Slave named Malissa aged fifteen years worth twenty five hundred dollars and that he has been deprived of her possession by James Wallace, Jesse A. Baker & Mary Baker his wife, Sarah Wallace, Margaret Cochran, & Lydia Wallace without his permission or consent.
P.A. Hodges
Sworn to and subscribed before me Jany 4th 1863
Jennings B. Kerr Clerk SC

State of North Carolina }
Mecklenburg County }

Know all men by these presents that we Patrick A. Hodges & **[Blank]** are held and firmly bound unto James Wallace, Jesse A. Baker & Mary his wife, Sarah Wallace, Margaret Cochran & Lydia Wallace in the sum of five thousand dollars - Witness their hands & seals July 4th 1864.

The condition of the above obligation is such whereas the above bounden Patrick A. Hodges hath sued out of the Superior Court of Law for said County against the said obligees a suit of neplurit for the recovery of a negro girl named Malissa aged fifteen years worth twenty five hundred dollars, and that he hath been deprived of the possession or consent, of by James Wallace, Jesse A. Baker & Mary his wife, Margaret Cochran Sarah Wallace and Lydia Wallace, And the said Patrick A. Hodges having given bond as the laws directs payable to the said James Wallace, Jesse A. Baker & Mary his wife, Sarah Wallace, Margaret Cochran & Lydia Wallace in the sum of five thousand dollars conditional to abide by and perform the Judgment of the Court.

These are therefore to command you to seize the said negro Slave Malissa if to be found in your County and deliver her to the possession of the said Patrick A. Hodges - Unless the said James Wallace, Jesse A. Baker & Mary his wife, Sarah Wallace, Margaret Cochran & Lydia Wallace shall execute and deliver to you a bond with sufficient security in the sum of five thousand dollars payable to the said Patrick A. Hodges and Conditional to perform the final Judgment of the Court - You are also commanded to summon the said James Wallace, Jesse A. Baker & Mary his wife, Sarah Wallace, Margaret Cochran & Lydia Wallace to appear before the Judge of our Superior Court of Law at the next Court to be held for the County of Mecklenburg at the Court House in Charlotte on the 11th Monday after the 4th Monday of February next then and there to answer the said Patrick A. Hodges of the said plea when and where you will make known how you have executed this suit - herein fail not & have you then and there this suit.
Witness Jennings B. Kerr Clerk of our said Court at Office the 11th Monday after the 4th Monday of August 1863.
Issued Jany 4th 1864 JB Kerr Clerk Sc

****

Barringer Vs. Shaw[?] & Elliott [1867]
Civil Action
Mecklenburg County

State of North Carolina }
Mecklenburg County } In the Superior Court

D.M. Barringer, Plaintiff
Against
R. Shaw & T.B. Elliott

The Complaint in this Case Shows:

I. That on the 1st day of Jany 1864 the said Defendant made a certain sealed note thereby promising to pay him the 1st of Sep 1865 to the Plaintiff three hundred dollars.

II. The 1st of Jany 1865 they made [?] sealed note, thereby promising to pay the Plaintiff eight hundred dollars.

III. That said note was given to the hire & services of a slave the property of the plaintiffs for the year 1864 & 1865 before the time said slave was emancipated.

That there is due thereon the sum of $210.00 with interest therein for the 1st of Jany 1865 for which judgment is demanded, with the costs of this action.
Ch[?] & Barringer Attorneys

R. Barringer, Attorney for the Plaintiff makes oath that this complaint is true as to all matters in his own knowledge he is informed and believes to be true; and that the claim sued on is in his possession.

Sworn to and subscribed before me this 22 day of April 186[?]
R. Barringer
Service of pleadings and notices may be made on the undersigned at Charlotte. R. Barringer, Attorney

We agree to pay the defendant Two Hundred Dollars, to be void, if the Plaintiff pay all costs the Defendant may recover in this action.
R. Barringer (Seal)

State of North Carolina
D.M. Barringer, Plaintiff
against
R. Shaw[?] & T.B. Elliot, Defendants
Mecklenburg County Superior Court

To the Sheriff of Mecklenburg County -- Greetings

You are hereby commanded, in the name of the State, to summon R. Shaw & T.B. Elliot to appear at the next on the 8th Monday after the 3rd Monday of March 1867, then and there to answer the complaint of D.M. Barringer, Plaintiff in this suit. And you are further commanded to notify the said defendant that if they fail to answer the said complaint, within the time specified, the said Plaintiff will demand Judgment for $200.00 with interest after the 1st day of Jany 1865 and for all costs and charges in this suit incurred.

Witness, E.A. Osborne, Clerk of the Superior Court, of Mecklenburg County, at Office in Charlotte, this the 22d day of April 1867.

We acknowledge ourselves bound unto the Defendant in this suit, in the sum of two hundred dollars, in case the Plaintiff fail in the prosecution thereof, to pay all costs, Etc., according to Act of Assembly
R. Barringer (Seal)

****

R.E. Cleveland Vs. Columbus Mills [1872]
Civil Action
Mecklenburg County

Mecklenburg County
Superior Court

R.E. Cleveland agst Columbus Mills

The plaintiff complains
I. That the Dft and one JH Carson on the 19th Novr. 1862 made their promissory note under seal by which they promised to pay T K **[?]** & NR Mills admrs of Govan Mills $ 232/.90 twelve months thereafter with interest from date.

II. That no part of said debt has ever been paid.

III. That afterward the said payees duly assigned & transferred the said note to the plaintiff for a valuable consideration.

Wherefore plaintiff demands judgment for said debt, interest & costs
Z B Vann Atto

Mecklenburg County
Superior Court

R.E. Cleveland, Plaintiff Vs. Columbus Mills, Defendant
Answer

The defendant answers to the Complaint

I. That the promissory note alleged to be due from the Defendant to the Plaintiff was given on the 19th of November 1862 for Confederate Money, and as such should be reduced to its real value in United States Currency.

II. That the said note was assigned and transferred to the Plaintiff in consideration of the payment of the amount of the note in Confederate States currency, and that no other consideration was received in the Assignment of said note.

III. That said note was given by the Defendant for the purchase of a negro slave: that said negro proved to be unsound and incapacitated by rheumatism to perform his work, and that the emancipation of said negro by the United States Government without any compensation therefore has deprived the Defendant of any valuable consideration received for the aforesaid note.

IV. The Defendant for further answer avers that he is not indebted to the Plaintiff in the amount claimed in the Complaint. That the property for which the aforesaid note was given was purchased by the Defendant at the sale of the Estate of Govan Mills, deceased; that he was charged by mistake with the purchase of a mule at said sale for the sum of **[not given]** that he did not purchase said mule and never received him; that the said amount of **[not given]** was added by error to the aforesaid note given by the Defendant, and that the said sum should be deducted from the Amount of the note claimed in the Complaint.
J.C. Mills, Deft. Atty

Columbus Mills being duly sworn says: I have read the foregoing answer and know the contents thereof.
The same is true of my own knowledge except as to Matters stated on information, and as to these I believe it to be true.
Columbus Mills
Sworn to before me this 29th day of May 1872
E.A. Osborne Test.

State of North Carolina } Superior Court
Mecklenburg County } Special Term

R E Cleveland against Columbus Mills

That at the time said Slave whose name was Paul was offered for sale, having been sold at publick Auction it was represented by the Vendor that said slave was sound and in addition there at, that he was a Carpenter by trade that the defendant noting upon the truthfulness of said explanations purchased said slave at the price of $1830 dollars when in truth and in fact said slave at that time was unsound, being afflicted by rheumatism and continued to be so afflicted until the time of his emancipation by [?] of which he was incapacitated to perform efficient labor - that in addition there at in truth and in fact he had no skill as a Carpenter nor was he qualified or competent to discharge the duties of a Carpenter - that the residue of said note was given in consideration of other property more fully appear by reference to exhibit 4, [?] made a part of this [?] with the exception of the charge therein for the mule, [?], of 85 dollars which charge was [?] therein through mistake as in [?] in the note

Wilson
Mills

****

Archibald Frew Vs. Alexander Hogan [1821]
Civil Action

Mecklenburg County

Archibald Frew } In the Superior Court of
Vs }
Alexander Hogan} Mecklenburg County North Carolina
Georgia Jasper County

By virtue of a Commission from the honorable the Superior Court of Mecklenburg County North Carolina to us directed we have caused George Hampton the person named in the said commission to come before us and being duly sworn true answers to make to certain interrogatories to the said annexed deposeth and answereth as follows.

Question 1st. Do you recollect to have levied executiory upon two negro slaves Mary and Joe & other property the property of David Cowan Senr. At the suit of Bryan and Schlatter & others, during the time you were Sheriff of Mecklenburg County?

Ansr. I do recollect that I did, and sold the said negroes & other property some time in the month of August 1811.

Q. 2nd. Did you sell the aforesaid negro slaves at fair and open sale by virtue of said executiory?

Ansr. I did sell them at fair and open sale and agreeable to law.

Q. 3rd. Who became the purchaser?

Ansr. They were bid off by William Flenniken who afterwards told me they were for Archibald Frew who would pay me the purchase money.

4th. Did A. Frew pay me the purchase money for said slaves and did you deliver them to him thereupon?

Ans. Archibald Frew did pay me the purchase money, no formal delivery was made, but I considered the slaves Archibald Frews on receiving the money from him.

Q. 5th. Do you recollect whether you gave to A. Frew a bill of sale for said slaves or not?

Ansr. I believe I did not.

Q. 6th. Do you recollect whether A. Frew did not let Mrs. Anne Cowan have the loan of the slaves Mary and Joe, and whether during the time you were Sheriff & residing in Mecklenburg they were not known and reputed to be his slaves.?

Ans. I know nothing of a loan, but I always believed them to be his slaves during the time I was Sheriff and afterwards.

Cross examined by the Attorney of Alexander Hogan
Q. 1st. Did not the slaves and sundry other articles bid off as the said sale, by William Flenniken & James Cowan remain in the possession and use of Mrs. Cowan after the sale thereof and during your stay in North Carolina?

Ansr. They did.

Q. 2nd. Do you know of Mr. A. Frew ever exercising any acts of ownership over the said slaves?

Ansr. I don't know that he ever did.

Answered subscribed, and submitted before us at the Court house in Monticello, Jasper County Georgia -- this 5th day of October 1821.
Geo Hampton
In presence of
Jesse Loyall JP (Seal)
John C. Gibson JP (Seal)

****

Andrew Walker Vs. John Patterson & others [1820]
Civil Action
Mecklenburg County

North Carolina } Equity - Novr. Term 1820
Mecklenburg County }

Andrew Walker
Vs
John Patterson & Others

In obedience to an Order of Court to me directed requiring me to ascertain the Amount of hire of a certain Negro in dispute from the date of last report untill this time I caused Thomas Winchester to appear before me (Who had hired sd. Negro) & state the Amt. of each years hire which he did as follows Viz

A.D.	1819	$115
	1820	$126
	1821	$124

The last Report stated the hire untill Octr. 1819 - the balance of that year Viz. 4 months would be, at $115

Pr. Annum	$38.33 1/3
AD 1820	$126
To the 1st May 1821 - At 124/ pr Annum	$41.33 1/3
	$205.66 2/3

****

Isaac Campbell Vs. William Alexander [1811]
Civil Action
Mecklenburg County

State of No. Carolina }
Mecklenburg County } Court of Equity

To William Alexander
and to the Sheriff of Mecklenburg County Greetings

For Certain Causes offered before us in our Court of Equity We Command and Strictly join you that Laying all Matters aside and Not

Withstanding any Excuse you Personally be and appeare before the Judge of our Superior Court of Equity for the County aforesaid at the Court House in Charlotte on the sixth Monday after the 4th Monday in September Next to answer Concerning those things Which Shall then and there be objected to you by Isaac Campbell in a bill of Complaint exhibited against you a Copy of which Said Bill of Complaint Accompanies this Writ, and to do further and receive whatsoever Said Court Shall have Considered in behalf and this you May in no wise omit under the Penalty of one Hundred Pounds & have you then this Writ of our said Court.

Witness Andw. McBride Clerk Master of our Said Court at office this 17 day of June 1811 and in the 35 year of our Independence.
Issued the 17 of June 1811
A. McBride C. & M. Eqty.

Isaac Campbell Vs Wm. Alexander

In this Case it is finally ordered & deemed by the Court that unless the deft. pay to the Complt. the sum of $150 together with the interest thereon or before the ninth day of September next the Equity of Redemption of the negroes from being the same mentioned in the mortgage & a Compt. Bill be and the same remain **[?]** and that the deft. pay all costs.

Isaac Campbell } In Equity
Vs
William Alexander }

Decree Principal	$150
Interest from Augt. 10, 1810	
to May 26 1812	$16.12½
	$166.12½

Costs Viz
One Copy of Bill 6 2/3 Copy sheets

at 2/each	$1.33
Subp.	$1
[?]	.20
fifa	$1
Enrolling bill	.33
Enrolling Decree 1 copy sheet	.40
	$5.26 } 28.26
Shff	1
State Tax	2
WP	20
	$28.26 } $194.38 1/2

Isaac Campbell Vs. William Alexander
In Equity

[?] principal	$150.00
Interest from August	
to May 26, 1812	16.12½
	166.12½
One Copy of a bill 6 2/3 Copy sheets	
a 2/each	1.33
[?] p.	1.00
Admission	.20
ffa	.37½
Enrolling Bill	1.33
Enrolling [?]	.40
	5.63½
Sheriff	1
State Tax	2
Acct	20
	28.63½
	194.76
	.37½
	195.13½

S. Bevens M.C. in Equity

June 15, 1812 recd. of Simeon Bevens - four dollars the Amount of my tax fee in the within case. A. McBride

June 15, 1812 recd. of Simeon Bevens one dollar at the Amount of my tax fees in the within case Geo. Hampton Shff

****

Johnson Clark & Co. Vs. D.G. Maxwell & J.T. Butler [1883]
Civil Action
Mecklenburg County

Superior Court, Mecklenburg County
Feby Term 1883

Johnson & Co. Plaintiffs
against
D G Maxwell & J T Butler

This case coming on to be heard upon the Certificate of the Supreme Court.

It is now on motion of Jones [?] & Johnston Attys for Plaintiff adjudged and declared. . that the Judgment heretofore rendered in the Superior Court be affirmed and same is the Judgment of the Court - with the interest and costs to be taxed by the Clerk of this Court

It is further adjudged that the plaintiff recover Judgment against surety on the Appeal bond for the costs of appeal

Jas C. Mac Rae, Judge &c

Chapter Two

Mecklenburg County

Criminal Actions

State Vs. Alexander Bigurt [1842]
Criminal Action
Trading with a Slave
Mecklenburg County

State of N. Carolina } Court of Pleas and Quarter Sessions
Mecklenburg County } April Term, 1842

The Jurors for the State upon their oath present that Alexander Bigart late of said County on the 23d day of April 1842 - with force and arms in said County - did unlawfully and wilfully sell and deliver to a certain slave named Charles the property of A.R. Gwin of said County - a quantity of spiritous liquors - viz - a pint or more - Contrary to the statute in such Case made and provided and against the peace and dignity of the State.

W.J. Davidson, Sol.

****

State Vs. Amos Reed, a free Negro [1841]
Criminal Action
Mecklenburg County

State of north Carolina.
To the Sheriff of Mecklenburg County -- Greeting:

Mecklenburg County

You are Hereby commanded to Summon James McNeely personally to be and appear before the Justices of our County Court of Pleas and Quarter Sessions, at the next Court to be held for said County, at the Courthouse in Charlotte, on the fourth Monday in April next, then and there to testify and the truth to say, in behalf of the State in a certain matter of controversy before the said Court depending, and then and there to be tried, wherein the State is Plaintiff, and Amos Reid a free negro is Defendant. And this you shall in no wise omit, under the penalty prescribed by law:

And this you shall in no wise omit, under the penalty prescribed by law:

Witness, Chas. T. Alexander, Clerk of our said Court, at Office the 4th Monday of October and in the sixty 66th year of our Independence, A.D. 1841

C.T. Alexander CCC

State of North Carolina

To the Sheriff of Mecklenburg County, Greeting:

You are hereby commanded to Summon Edwin L. Alexander personally to be and appear before the Justices of our County Court of Pleas and Quarter Sessions, at the next Court to be held for said County, at the Courthouse in Charlotte, on the fourth Monday in April next, then and there to testify and the truth to say, in behalf of the State in a certain matter of controversy before the said Court depending, and then and there to be tried, wherein the State is Plaintiff, and Amos Reed a free Negro is Defendant.

And this you in no wise omit, under the penalty prescribed by law.

Witness, Chas. T. Alexander, Clerk of our said Court, at Office the 4th Monday of October and in the 66th year of our Independence, A.D. 1841

C.T. Alexander CCC

****

State Vs. William A. Todd [1842]
Criminal Action
Trading with a Slave
Mecklenburg County

State of N. Carolina } Court of Pleas and Quarter Sessions
Mecklenburg County } April Term 1842

The Jurors for the State upon their oath present that Wm. A. Todd late of Said County on the 28 day of April 1842 with force and Arms in Said County did sell and deliver to a Certain Slave named Bonhart the property of Jas. M. Hutchinson's estate. A quantity of Merchandise to wit, 1 Pr of Gloves Contrary to the statute in Sutch Case made & provided, And against the peace And dignity of the State.
W.F. Davidson, Sol.

****

State Vs. Evan Hagler, Free man of Color [1841]
Criminal Actions
Assault & Battery
Mecklenburg County

State of North Carolina } To any Constable or Lawful
Mecklenburg County } officer to Execute & return

Whereas complaint hath been made before me J.B. Kerr one of the Justices of the peace in & for said County upon the Oath of Jno Cashion in said County that Evan Hagler Blacksmith (Colored) a free man of Color did on the 12th Nov. 1841 violently assault and beat him the said John Cashion in the Town of Charlotte in the County aforesaid.

These are therefore to Command you forthwith to apprehend the said Evan Hagler (Free man of Color) and to bring him before me or some other Justice of the peace for the said County to answer the Said Complaint and to be further dealt with according to Law.

Given under my hand & seal the 12th day of Nov. 1841
J B Kerr JP (Seal)

Mecklenburg County

State Vs. E Hagler
Warrant - A & B, Executed
Jesse W Harris

State of North Carolina }
Mecklenburg County }

The defendant & H C **[?]** & S.A. Harris acknowledge themselves indebted to the State of North Carolina in the sum of Fifty dollars Each to be levied of their goods and chattles, lands & Tenaments to be void on condition that Evan Hagler make his personal appearance at the next Court of Pleas & Quarter sessions to be held for said County on the 4th Monday in April next: Witness our hands & Seals this 12 Nov. 1841

N.W. Alexander J.P. his
Evan X Hagler (Seal)
mark

S A Harris & H C **[Torn]**

****

State Vs. M. Barry & J. Dwyer [1864]
Criminal Action
Felony (Stealing)
Mecklenburg County

North Carolina } Court of Pleas & Quarter Sessions
Mecklenburg County } Jany T. 1864

The Jurors for the State upon their Oath present:

That M. Barry, James Dwyer, and James Young, a free person of Color, late of the County of Mecklenburg on the 11th day of January, Anno Domini, One thousand Eight Hundred & Sixty four, in the Value of Ten Dollars, of the goods & of John Wilkes then and there being found, feloniously did steal, take and drive away -- & the jurors for the State upon their Oath do further present that M. Barry and James Dwyer late of the County of Mecklenburg on the 11th day of January One Thousand Eight Hundred & Sixty four in the County aforesaid Ten pounds of Beef of the value five dollars and one Cow & skin both of the goods & chattles

of Jno Wilkes of the value of Five dollars feloniously did receive from one James Young, a free man of Color, knowing the same to have been stolen, contrary to the statute in such case made & provided and against the peace & dignity of the State.
J M Hutchison, Sol.

North Carolina } Court of Pleas & Quarter Sessions
Mecklenburg County } Jany Term 1864

M. Barry maketh Oath that he is advised & believes that Adeline Stanly will be a material witness for him upon the Trial of his Suit. He expects to prove by sd. Witness that about Eleven O'Clock on the day the cow alleged to have been stolen was butchered, that the negro James Young was reputed to be a free negro, came to affiant, and Employed him to take his waggon & [?] to Major Morrows, and bring in the beef [?] for him. that he promised to pay affiant five dollars for his services in sd doings, That in pursuance of the Contract to this affiant went with sd negro to Major Morrows & got the Beef [?] That the Beef was brought to [?] & sold by the negro & That affiant got no part of the money & that the negro asked affiant to sell the hide for him & take his pay, To wit, five dollars for his services in the matter, out of the proceeds of the sale of the hide, wherein he did & that sd. Witness is confined to her bed with sickness, and is unable to attend Court; as affiant is [?] & [?].
Wm. Maxwell CLC his
M. X Barry
mark

****

State Vs. Minerva Smith, Free Woman of Color [1859]
Criminal Action
Mecklenburg County

State of North Carolina
To the Sheriff of Mecklenburg County -- Greeting

We command you, that of the Goods and Chattels, Lands and Tenements of Minerva Smith (free woman of Color) if to be found in your bailiwick, you cause to be made the sum of twenty five dollars for fine which was lately in our Court of Pleas and Quarter Sessions, held for Mecklenburg county, at the Court house in Charlotte, adjudged The State for costs and charges in the said suit expended, whereof the said Minerva Smith is liable, as appears to us of record. And have you the said moneys, besides your fees for this service, before our said Court at Charlotte aforesaid, on the 4th Monday in April next, then and there to render the said Court the debt, interest, costs and charges aforesaid. Herein fail not; and have you then and there this writ.

Witness, William K. Reid, Clerk of our said Court, at Office, the 4th Monday in January A.D. 1859, and in the 83 year of American Independence. Issued the 16th day of Feby. 1859.
W.K. Reid CCC

State of North Carolina
To the Sheriff of Mecklenburg County -- Greeting

We command you, as we have before commanded you, that of the Goods and Chattels, Lands and Tenements of Minerva Smith (free woman of color) if to be found in your bailiwick, you cause to be made the sum of Twenty five dollars for fine which was lately in our Court of Pleas and Quarter Sessions, held for Mecklenburg county, at the Court House in Charlotte, adjudged The State for costs and charges in the said suit expended, whereof the said Minerva Smith is liable, as appears to us of record. And have you the said moneys, besides your fees for this service, before our said Court at Charlotte aforesaid, on the 4th Monday in July next, then and there to render the said Court the costs and charges aforesaid. Herein fail not; and have you then and there this writ.

Witness, William K. Reid, Clerk of our said Court, at Office, the 4th Monday in April A.D. 1859 and in the 83 year of American Independence. Issued the April 24th day of May 1859.
W.K. Reid

State of North Carolina
To the Sheriff of Mecklenburg County -- Greeting.

We command you, as we have oftentimes before commanded you, that of the Goods and Chattels, Lands and Tenements of Minerva Smith (free woman of color) if to be found in your bailiwick, you cause to be made the sum of Twenty five dollars for fine which was lately in our Court of Pleas and Quarter Sessions, held for Mecklenburg county, at the Court House in Charlotte, adjudged The State for costs and charges in the said suit expended, whereof the said Minerva Smith is liable, as appears to us of record. And have you the said moneys, besides your fees for this service, before our said Court at Charlotte aforesaid, on the 4th Monday in October next, then and there to render the said Court the fine, costs and charges aforesaid. Herein fail not; and have you then and there this writ.

Witness, William K. Reid, Clerk of our said Court, at Office the 4th Monday in July A.D. 1859, and in the 84 year of American Independence. Issued 22 day of August 1859.
W.K. Reid

State of North Carolina.
To the Sheriff of Mecklenburg County -- Greeting

We command you, as we oftentimes before commanded you, that of the Goods and Chattels, Lands and Tenements of Minerva Smith (free woman of color) if to be found in your bailiwick, you cause to be made the sum of Twenty five dollars for fine which was lately in our Court of Pleas and Quarter Sessions, held for Mecklenburg county, at the Court House in Charlotte, adjudged the State also the sum of Seventeen & 20/100 dollars for costs and charges in the said suit expended, whereof the said Minerva Smith is liable, as appears to us of record. And have you the said moneys, besides your fees for this service, before our saod Court at Charlotte aforesaid, on the 4th Monday in January next, then and there to render the said Court the fine, costs and charges aforesaid. Herein fail not; and have you then and there this writ.

Witness, William K. Reid, Clerk of our said Court, at Office, the 4th Monday in October A.D. 1859, and in the 84 year of American Independence. issued the 19 day of November 1859.
W.K. Reid

****

State Vs. Joseph Baker [1873]
Criminal Action
Murder
Mecklenburg County

State of North Carolina
Tod R. Caldwell, Governor and Commander-in-Chief

To all who shall see these Presents--Greeting:

Whereas, Joseph Baker at the Spring Term, one thousand eight hundred and seventy three, of the Superior Court of Law of Mecklenburg County, was convicted of Murder, and by judgment of said Court was sentenced to be hanged Dec. 19, 1873, from which Sentence a respite was granted him until Friday, January 2, 1874.

Now therefore I, Tod R. Caldwell, Governor of the State of North Carolina, for sufficient causes me thereunto moving, and by virtue of the power and authority in me vested by the Constitution of the State, do hereby Reprieve the said Joseph Baker and grant him a further respite from the execution of said sentence until Friday the 16th day of January, A.D. 1874, when the Sheriff of Mecklenburg County will execute the said sentence as appointed by the Court and as the law directs.

In Witness Whereof, I have hereunto set my hand and caused the Great Seal of State to be affixed.

Done at our City of Raleigh, this the 2d day of January, in the year of our Lord one thousand eight hundred and seventy-four, and in the ninety-eighth year of our Independence.
By the Governor Tod R. Caldwell (Great Seal of State)
D Meatheny**[?]**, Private Secretary

****

State Vs. Simon, a Negro [1793]
Criminal Action
Felony (Stealing)
Mecklenburg County

State of North Carolina
Mecklenburg County

State Vs Simon, A Negroe who calls himself the property of Thos. Wade. Charged with Horse Stealing & Robbery.

On the Trial of Said Simon Robert Irwin, Thomas Alexander & George Graham Justices, and Charles Roth Junr., Richard Moser, Robert Allison and John Wilson (the Jury), which said Justices and Freeholders being duly sworn, and on Hearing sd. Simon examined says that he took a Horse Creature, but thought it was his own, and being accused with robbing a house of Sundry articles acknowledges he did take out of a House the following articles Viz. A Blue Coat. A Cottin homespun gown. A Black Petticoat and a pair of Breeches.

James Rogers a witness -- says his Negroe fellow alarmed him on Tuesday said his House was robbed by a Negroe fellow, he raised a party and pursued but could not find, a few days after he met a Negroe and took him, he made his escape &c that Monday morning following, being the 22nd July A Negro was taken at Robt. Glass's, Mr Rogers got the several artickles that his house was robbed of, being the same that the above Simon Confesses to takeing out of a House.

Zebulon Ford says on Saturday the 20th July he missed A Horse Creature of his from the rest, that on Monday following Negroe Simon was taken at Mr. Robt. Glass's who had Mr. Foards Creature in custody, and that Mr. Roger's Cloaths above described was also found in his custody. B **[Name Smeared]** A Negroe fellow a witness, being charged, says, that on Tuesday he was at work his Master and Mistress being from home he had shut the Door open, saw a black Man come out of the House wt. his Masters Coat &c, come towards him & hollowed to him he wanted a coat - that he told him to come there & get it, & rode on.

On hearing the Testimony aforesaid and duly deliberating thereon it is the oppinion of us the Justices and Freeholders aforesaid that the said Negro Simon shall remain in close confinement, untill Thursday the eighth day of August 1793 and from his said place of confinement between the Hour of 12 & 4 Oclock in the afternoon of said day be taken to the place of Execution By the Sheriff, or other proper officer and there be hanged by the Neck untill he is dead. Dead

Witness our Hands this 30th Day of July 1793
Tryal of Simeon, Negroe, July 30th 1793

Robt. Irwin, JP, John Foard, JP, Geo Graham, JP, Thos. Alexander, JP, Richd Moser, Cha. Roth, Robert Allison & John Wilson.

****

State Vs. Negro Dick [1791]
Criminal Action
Felony (Stealing)
Mecklenburg County

State of North Carolina }
Mecklenburg County }

To any Sworn officer Sheriff or Constable Greeting:
This Day William McCullock appeared Before us James Tagert & Wm. Wilson Justices of the peace for the Said County & Complains on oath that about four years ago he Said McCulloch had stolen from him & feloniously Carried away Sundry Goods & Clothing Viz. three linning Shurts one or more pairs of overals one peticote & Short womans Gound with Sundry other artickles Both of Men & womens wear or clothing & that hee has Now raison from the Information of a Certain Negro fellow Called Dick to Judge a Negro fellow Called Tom Peterson Negro of William Peterson for taking Said Clothing as said Dick confesses he was with the said Tom when taken & that he this Deponents people found some artickles of Said Clothing the Same way that Said Dick Says they went with Said Stolen property & this Deponent further Saith that he then at the time the said Goods was stolen Computed the whole to Be of the value of five pounds this Currency, This is therefore to Command you to apprehend the Said Negros Called Tom & Dick & them if to be found have Before us or Some other Justices of the peace for Said County Now in Charlote against three Oclock this afternoon & this Shall be your warrant Given under our hands & Seals this 4th Day of February 1791.

James Tagert (Seal)
Wm Wilson (Seal)

You are Required if the Negro Tom is taken to Give his Master William Petterson Notice to attend on hid behalf[?]

State of North Carolina }
Mecklenburg County }

At a Court of Justices & Freeholders Legally Summoned for the Tryal of a certain Negro man Slave Named Dick (the property of **[Blank]**) & duly begun & held at the Court House in sd. County on the fourth day of February in the year of our Lord one thousand seven Hundred & Ninety One & in the XV Year of Independence.
Present
The Worshipful Hezekiah Alexander, John Mck Alexander & William Polk, Justices assigned to keep the peace for said County

Messrs John Springs, Thomas Grier, Richard Mason, Robert Barnett & Saml. McCombs, Freeholders owners of slaves.

The said Justices & freeholders are Sworn [?] & truly to Try the said Negro Man Slave named Dick now a prisoner at the bar.

The said Negro man Slave named Dick Charged with Burglary & fellony that he the said Dick on the Second day of February 1791 did Brake open William McColloh House & from Thence did take out & Steal & Carry away of the Goods & Chattles of sd. William McCulloh to the Value of five shillings Sterling William McCulloh Evidence against the Prisoner at the Bar towit Negro man Slave Dick, Deposeth on His Oath Saith that on the 2d. Day February the said Deponent missed sundry artickles out of his House & In His suspecting the aforesaid Negro Man Slave Dick Did pursue the Said Negro Dick & found in his Possession Sundrie of his Said Goods in the Said Negro Dicks possession.

And upon the Confession of the Prisoner at the bar and sundry other evidences fully proven the said facts it is therefore Considered by the Court that the Said Negro Man Slave Dick is Guilty of Stealing and

Burglary as before charged against him & shall be conveyed from the Bar to the Common gaol of the County & there remain untill Thursday next & from thence to the place of Execution at 2 Oclock and there to be hanged by the Neck untill he be Dead.

Justices - owners of Slaves: Hez. Alexander, Wm. Polk & J Mck Alexander.

Freeholders - owners of Slaves: John Springs, Thos. Grier, Richd Mason, Sam McCombs & Robert Barnet.

****

State Vs. Peter, a Negro Man [1786]
Criminal Action
Mecklenburg County

The State Vs. Peter a Negro Man} (Copy) Habs. Corpus

E.H. Bay

Mr. William Massey
You are hereby Served with a Copy of this Writ of Habeas Corpus to the Intent that you may immediately appear on the Return thereof before the Honbl. Aedanus Burke Esquire to show Cause if any you have Why the within named Negro Man Peter should not be Set at Liberty.
E.H. Bay Atty

South Carolina To Hugh Milling Esquire Sheriff of Camden District, or to any of his lawful Deputies in Said District Greeting:

You are hereby commanded that you have the Body of Peter a negro man detained in the custody of one William Massey as it is said by whatever name he is called in the same, together with the day and the Cause of the taking and detaining the Said Peter before the Justices of the State aforesaid at their Chambers in Camden aforesaid immediately after the Receipt of this Writ to do and receive what the said Justices shall then and there consider of him in his behalf. And have you then and there this writ.

Witness the Honourable Aedanus Burke Esquire one of the aforesaid Justices of the State aforesaid at Camden this twenty ninth day of April in the year of our Lord one thousand seven Hundred and eighty Six, and in the Tenth year of American Independence.

Know all Men by these Presents that I Joseph Caryl of the state of South Carolina & Camden District have made ordained & appointed William Massey of the Sd. State & Sd. District My Lawful Attorney for me and in my Name and to my Use to ask & Demand and Execute All such sum or sums of Money as May appear Due to me from any Person or Persons Whatever for the time that I Lay out the use of my Negro Peter Which was from the twenty fifth Day of July one thousand seven hundred and Eighty five untill the Nineteenth Day of January Eighty six a good and sufficient Discharge for me and in my Name to give and Execute for the same in Witness Whereof I set my Hand and fix my seal this 20th Day of Jany. 1786.
Signed sealed and Delivered
William Crook Junior
William Taylor

To all to whom these Presents Shall Come I Joseph Caryl Do Send Greeting Know ye that I the sd. Joseph Caryl of the State of South Carra. & County of Lanckester for & in Consideration of the Sum of forty Pounds Sterling have bargained & Sold unto William Massey his heirs exrs Admrs. one Negro fellow Named Peter now being in my Present Possession Before the Signing of these Presents I have Delivered him the Sd. Negro fellow Peter unto the Sd. Wm. Massey his heirs Exrs or Admrs from hence forth as his or Theirs **[Torn]** Proper Right & title without **[Torn]** manor of Condition I the Sd. Joseph Caryl Do forever Defend the Right & title of the sd. Negro unto the Sd. Wm. Massey his heirs Exrs. or Admrs. in Witness whereof I have hereunto Set my hand & Seal this 20th Day of January 1786.
Joseph Caryl (Seal)

Test
Jas. Massey
William Crook Junior

[Top line torn] Rives
[Torn] has Received of Ann Young
To Run on Interest until paid

[Torn] Say Received this **[Blank]** Day of **[Blank]** 1785
Witness William Rives
James Massey

April 28 the Ballance due upon the Bill of 1786 scasle**[?]** To William Massey is is £7-16-9

July 24 1792 Rec'd of James Tagert Admr. of the within Seven pounds North Carolina Currency **[?]** me William Massey

March the 25 Joseph Caryl
1790 By Nineteen shillings procl.
paid By Richard Mason £3

J.F. Grimkes
£30.0.0
South Carolina
The State of South Carolina, To all and singular the Sheriffs of the said State, Greeting: You and each of You are hereby commanded without Delay, that of the Goods and Chattels, Houses, Lands, and other Hereditaments, and real Estates of William Massey you cause to be levied the Sum of Eighteen pounds six shillings and three pence sterling which Archibald Davie guardian of a certain free Negro called Peter in the Court of Common Pleas, before the Justices of the said Court at Camden lately recovered against the said William for his damages sustained for the unlawful detaining and imprisoning the said Negro Peter and for his Costs and Charges by Him expended in and about prosecuting his Suit in that Behalf, Whereof the said William Stands convicted, as appears on Record.

And that you have the Money before the said Justices at the said Court of Common Pleas, to be holden at Charleston, on the **[Blank]** Tuesday in **[Blank]** next, to render the said Archibald for his Damages, Costs and Charges aforesaid. And have you then and there this Writ. Witness the Honorable John F. Grimke Esquire one of the Associate Justices at Charleston, the **[Blank]** Day of **[Blank]** in the Year of our Lord One Thousand Seven Hundred and Eighty seven in the Eleventh Year of the Sovereignty and Independence of the United States of America.
E:H: Bay Plffs's Atty:

Rec'd July 24th 1792 of James Tager Admr. the Sum of Thirty pounds which Included seven pounds **[?]** on the Bill of sale the whole Debt **[?]** and Interest Due me William Massey

Camden
Archibald Davie Vs. William Massey: Fe Fa
Entd. in office 7th Feby., H Melling
E:H: Bay
Levy Dams: & Costs: £18.6.3, not subject to the Installment Law

Novr. the 22d day 1788 Seven pounds Eighteen Shillings and **[?]** Pence His interest of this **[Faded]** William Massey

****

State Vs. Mariah Bone[1864]
Criminal Action
Trading with a Slave
Mecklenburg County

North Carolina 1864 } Court of Pleas & quarter
Mecklenburg County } Sessions Jany Term 1864

The Jurors for the State upon their Oath present

Mecklenburg County

That Mariah Bone - late of the County of Mecklenburg on this 11th day of January in the Year of our Lord one Thousand Eight Hundred and Sixty four in the County aforesaid did unlawfully purchase between the hours of sun set and sun rise a parcel of wood, to wit., three Sticks, from Romulus a slave, the property of R.M. Jamiston of the County aforesaid: & the jurors for the state upon their Oath do further present that the said Mariah Bone did on the day aforesaid between the hours of sun set & sun rise, receive a parcel of wood, to wit, three sticks from Romulus - a Slave, the property of R.M. Jamison, Knowing the same to have been stolen, against the Statute in such case made & provided & against the Peace & dignity of the State.
JM Hutchison, Solicitor

****

State Vs. Jo, a Slave [1841]
Criminal Action
Mecklenburg County

State of North Carolina
To the Sheriff of Mecklenburg County --- Greeting:
You are hereby commanded to Summon Samuel Watson personally to be and appear before the Justices of our County Court of Pleas and Quarter Sessions, at the next Court to be held for said County, at the Courthouse in Charlotte, on the fourth Monday in April next, then and there to testify, and the truth to say, in behalf of the State in a certain matter of controversy before said Court depending, and then and there to be tried, wherein the State is Plaintiff, and Jo the slave of Samuel Watson is Defendant. And this you shall in no wise omit, under the penalty prescribed by law.

Witness, Chas. T. Alexander, Clerk of our said Court at Office the 4th Monday of October and in the sixty 6th year of our Independence, A.D. 1841.
C.T. Alexander CCC

State of North Carolina
To the Sheriff of Mecklenburg County --- Greeting:

Mecklenburg County

You are hereby commanded to Summon John N. Lee personally to be and appear before the justices of our County Court of Pleas and Quarter Sessions, at the next Court to be held for said County, at the Courthouse in Charlotte, on the fourth Monday in April next, then and there to testify, and the truth to say, in behalf of the State in a certain matter of controversy before said Court depending, and then and there to be tried, wherein the State is Plaintiff, and Jo the Slave of Samuel Watson is Defendant. And this you shall in no wise omit, under the penalty prescribed by law.

Witness, Chas. T. Alexander, Clerk of our said Court at Office the 4th Monday of October and in the sixty 6th year of our Independence, A.D. 1841.
C.T. Alexander CCC

****

State Vs. Joe, a Slave [1806]
Criminal Action
Murder
Mecklenburg County

State of North Carolina }
Mecklenburg County }

At an intermediate Court convened at Charlotte on Wednesday the 24th day of December 1806 was present the Worshipful
Charles T. Alexander }
Adam A. Springs } Esquires
David Cowan }

When the Sheriff of Said County brought into Court a certain Negro Man Slave the property of Robert Wiley named Joe - Charged with the Murder of Bill also a Slàve the property of James Wilson Esqr. and the said Joe Being Charged pleads Not Guilty - whereupon the Court entered the following Jury Viz. Thomas Alexander, Ezekiel Black, John Black, George Hutchison, Robert Barnett, John B. Springs, John Robeson, James Robinson, Isaac Mcculloh, Geo Hampton (being all owners of Slaves) Impannelled & Sworn

State Vs Joe a Slave
To try the said Negro Joe (a Slave) after being Sworn in due & Solemn form of Law Do upon their Oaths find and say that the Negro Joe is Guilty of Man Slaughter.

Ordered by the Court that the Said Joe be branded on his left cheek with **the letter M & that the brand shall be of sufficiently Deep to make a** lasting impression.
by the Sheriff — Adam A. Springs JP
Da. Cowan JP

****

State Vs. Nathan, a Slave [1807]
Criminal Action
Felony (Stealing)
Mecklenburg County

State of N. Carolina } To the Sheriff of said County
Mecklenburg County } or to the Keeper of the Common

Jail of said County - I send you herewith the Body of a Negro fellow Named Nathan belonging to Daniel Gallant of sd. County, who being taken on my Warrant and brought before me Charged with Stealing Sundry Store Goods at Different times out of a Store House belonging to sd. Gallant which Store House is now Occupied by Bartlett Meacham the owner of the sd. Goods Stolen - the goods are said on Oath to be Stolen part of them on the night of the Thursday of the last Court week in sd. County, and part of them Stolen since but the precise time not known, and are, two peaces of Nankean, a Remnant of Linen, Some Kneedles, some Rum, four pair shoes and twelve Dollars - whereupon the sd. Negro Nathan hath been duly examined by me and he Voluntarily Confessed that he did enter the store House of sd. Meacham (by opening the Door with a Kee which he said he found in the end of sd. Gallants Road) and stole out thence in the night time as many as three times since the last Court in said County the following Articles (to wit) two peaces of Nankeen, a piece of Linen, Some Kneedles and some Coffee and Seven Dollars in Cash - These are therefore to command you to receive the said Nathan into your custody in the Gaol of sd County there to Remain till he be delivered from

your Custody by the due Course of Law Given under my hand and seal in sd. County this 4th of July A.D. 1807.
Jno. Kendrick JP (Seal)
To Thomas Spratt, Charles Dewey[?], Joseph Smith - to Deliver to the Sheriff or Jailor - No Constable being handy.

State of N. Carolina }
Mecklenburg }

Whereas Bartlett Meacham hath Complained on Oath to me John Kendrick one of the Justices of the peace for sd. County that there hath been stolen from him out of a Store House belonging to Daniel Gallant in sd. County (Which House is now Occupyed by sd Meacham) on the Thursday night of the last April Court in this County the following Articles (to wit) four pair of Mens Shoes, Seven Dollars in Cash and a Remnant of Linen, and also that since that time there hath been also Stolen from him out of the Same House some Nankeen, Some Kneedles and some Rum (the quantity of either is not known) and five Dollars in Cash; and that he hath good Reason to believe that a Negroe fellow named Nathan, and two Negroe Women both by the name of Beck, all belonging to Daniel Gallant in sd. County, are the persons who hath stolen them - These are therefore in behalf of the State to command you to Search the Dwelling places of sd. Negroes and bring them before me, or some other Justice for sd. County to be examined upon the premises and to be dealt with according to law - and if you find the sd. Goods, or any of them to Secure them and bring them forward at the same time with the sd. Negroes, herein fail not - make Due Return in thirty days and this is your Warrant given under my hand at my own House in sd. County this 3rd July A.D. 1807.
Jno. Kendrick JP
To Henry Meacham to Execute.

State of N. Carolina }
Mecklenburg County }

This day Bartlett Meacham personally came before me John Kendrick one of the Justices of the peace for sd. County and made Oath that there hath been Stolen from him out of a Store House belonging to Daniel Gallant Now occupyed by sd. Meacham in the County aforesd on the Thursday night of the April Court in sd. County 1807 four pair of Men's Shoes, Seven Dollars in Cash, and a Remnant of Linen and also since that time hath been Stolen from him out of the same House Some Nankeen, some Needles and some Rum, also five Dollars in Cash (the quantity of the goods is not known but thought to be worth Thirty Dollars) And that he hath Sufficient Reason to believe that a Negro fellow belonging to Daniel Gallant Named Nathan in sd. County, and two Negroe Wenches also belonging to the sd. Gallant both by the Name of Beck are the very persons who Stole the sd. Goods.
Sworn to and Subscribed before me this 3rd July 1807.
Jno. Kendrick JP Bart. Meacham

State of North Carolina }
Mecklenburg County }

The Examination of A Negroe fellow Named Nathan belonging to Daniel Gallant in sd. County - And also of two Negroe Women belonging to sd. Gallant, both of them by the Name of Beck - They being taken on my Warrant and brought before me Charged with Stealing Sundry Store Good from Bartlett Meacham out of his Store in sd. County - The sd. Nathan Confessed before me that he had a key which he found in the Road, with which he could open the Door of sd. Store, and that he had entered the sd. Store Several times in the Night with sd. Key - And that the first time he went in Was about the time of the last court in this County - and that he took out of sd. Store in the Whole, at the Different times the following Articles (to wit) The sd. Nathan Says he took two peaces of Nankeen, a peace of Linen, Seven Dollars in Money, Some Kneedles, some Coffee & Some Rum - The two Wenches Confessed nothing, and no evidence appearing against them are therefore Discharged - Taken before me at my own House in the County aforesaid this 4th July A.D. 1807.
Jno. Kendrick JP

State of North Carolina }

Mecklenburg County }

Be it remembered that on the 4th day July in the year of our Lord One Thousand Eight Hundred Seven Barcklet Mitchem Merchant in Said County, personally Came Before Me John Kindrick one of the Justices of the peace in Said County And Acknowledged Him self to Owe to the Estate of North Carolina the Sum of One Hundred pounds Current Money of said State to be levied of his goods And Chattels to the Use of the said State if he the Said Barklit Mitcham Shall fail in the Condition underwritten.

The Condition of the Above recognizance is such that if the Above Bound Barklit Mitcham Doth Appear At the Court House for said County on Friday of the July Term next or Sooner if required to give evidence in Behalf of the State Against A negro fellow Belonging to Daniel Gallant named Nathin in a Charge against Said Nathin for Stealing Sundrys Store goods from him sd. Barklit Mitcham then the Above recognizance to be Void if not to remain in full force and Virtue.
Acknowledged before me Bart. Meacham
Jno Kendrick JP

To William Berryhill
Sir I hereby Depute you to Summon

Thomas Greer, James Tigert & Michl McLary Esquires to form a special Court.

Capt. Saml. Neel, Maj. David Hartt, William Ferguson, Hugh Parks, Joseph McCrumb, James McKnight, Andrew McNeely, Samuel McCrumb, John Springs Senr., William Flennigan, Geo. Graham & Jessey Clark

as jurors, all to meet at the Court House in Charlotte on Tuesday the 21st Instant to try an action, the State against Danl. Gallant's negro slave Nathan
J.W.B. Sheriff
July 18th 1807

[?] Am sick and unable to ride - is to them to attend a Court 10 Oclock
J.W.B.

State of North Carolina

At an Intermediate Court began and held for the County of Mecklenburg at the Court House in Charlotte on the 21st day of July 1807.

Present the Worshipfull
Thomas Greer, Nichl. McClury, James Tegert, John Kendrick & David McDonald, Esquires

Jury - Samuel Neel, David Hart, William Ferguson, Hugh Parks, Joseph McCrum, John Springs Snr., William Flennikan, Geo Graham, Jesse Clark, Samuel McCrum, James McKnight and Samuel Berryhill.
Jury inpannelled & sworn

Bartlet Meacham Prst
State Vs. Nathan a Slave of or belonging to Daniel Gallant, Grand Larceny, Charged & pleads not Guilty.

Jury charged verdt. find the Defendt Nathan is not Guilty in Manner & form of Charges.

****

State Vs. Nathan , a Slave [1809]
Criminal Action
Felony (Stealing)
Mecklenburg County

State of North Carolina }
Mecklenburg County }

Personally appeared before us Jas. Sprott, John Kendrick and Will Casser Justices of the peace for sd. County - Will McRee, John Smith and Edmund Smith on behalf of the State against Nathan a Slave the property of Joshua Dinkins accused of feloniously taking away from the premises of Sd Will McRee Goods and Chattels to the amount of Seven dollars - Will Mcree Sworn Sayeth that a Hay fork which he lost last spring and a skillet which he lost the January preceeding - and is now present is his property and that he never had traded or gave away Sd property - and that the said property is worth for shilling currency of that State - Edmund Smith Sworn Sayeth that he saw the Skillet now present in possession of the Slave Nathan about the middle of Janr. 1809 - also that he saw the Hay fork now present he saw in the possession of the Slave Nathan Sometime about the middle of last summer - also that he took away sd fork from sd Slave and kept it until the present time.

Febr 8th 1810 — Wm McRee
Acknowledged before us — Emd. Smith
Will Casser JP — John Smith
Jas. Spratt Att: JP

****

State Vs. William Phillips [1841]
Criminal Actions
Trading with a Slave
Mecklenburg County

State of North Carolina } Court of Pleas and Quarter Sessions
Mecklenburg County } October Term 1841

The Jurors for the State upon their oath present that William Phillips late of said County on the 23d day of October A.D. 1841 - with force and arms in said County did then and there unlawfully sell and deliver to a certain negro slave named Mose & Tim the property of John Irwin of said County, a quantity of spiritous liquors to wit, a pint or more without an order in writing from their master contrary to the Statute in such case made and provided and against the peace and dignity of the State.
W.F. Davidson, Sol.

****

State Vs. Ben, Joe, & Sam, Slaves [1793]
Criminal Action
Felony (Stealing)
Mecklenburg County

Agreeably to an Act of the General Assembly we the undernamed Justices and Freeholders and owners of Slaves within the County of Mecklenburg being legally summoned by the Sheriff of the said County to try several Negro slaves agreeably to a Warrant granted under the hand and seal of Hezekiah Alexander one of the Justices for the said County, being convened at the House of Richard Mason in the Town of Charlotte first being legally sworn, have caused Frederick Shaver to come before us who being duly sworn deposeth and sayeth, that on Sunday the 21st day of the present month April 1793 he had feloniously taken from his Spring House one Keg of of Whiskey containing Ten gallons and upwards, that on information having been Rec'd that Ben, Negroe of Robert Phillips had been in his neighborhood on the said Sabbath day and of his going to Major Harris's and from thence home on the said Day he the sd. Frederick with his Son persued on towards Phillips on the back track of a Horse which had been stolen or missing on the said evening and did take the said Negroe Ben, who confessed when after tying him, he confessed that he was in the sd Shavers Neighborhood on the said Sabbath day & in company with the Negroes Sam & Joe the property of Ezekl. Black & Tunis Hood Senr., that on the said Bens proposing to go home to Majr. Harris's Sam told him he could get him a Horse to ride up in the woods, that he the said Ben did consent & that the said Ben, Joe & Sam did take the Horse which was said to be Tunis Shavers & that Joe held the Horse whilst Ben & Sam striped Bark & made a Halter which was put on - that Ben did then mount the Horse & was about to go on to Majr. Harris's when Sam told him to stop, and they would get some whiskey - it was asked where it could be had, it was answered by Sam, it could be had at Fred. Shavers Spring House - They all went back to the rock which crossed the creek, where Ben was left & Sam & Joe went on, but staying longer than was expected he Ben went on to Majr. Harris's when this deponent followed and was told by Mrs. Harris that the said Ben was there - that he the depn. followed to Phillips as aforesaid & was told by Alexander McClure, that he McClure was **[?]** on Monday morning following the said 21st.

Tunis Shaver on his oath declareth that the foregoing Deposition of Fred. Shaver which has been read to him is similar to what the said Fred. has sworn [?] as to what was heard at Majr. Harris's - And also furthermore sayeth that he in company with Capt. Tunis Hood did on the 22d. of the present instant go to the House of Ezekl. Black and take Negroe Sam & after carrying him into the lane where they were met by Fred. Shavers with Negroe Joe, after examination Sam did confess that he was aiding and assisting in taking the Horse & that he made the Sattles - And also that Sam enquired of Ben who was then present why he called his dog back when we were going down Yonder - Joe on examination declared that him & Sam went from the aforementioned Rock where they left Ben, to the Spring House for the Whiskey that Sam went into the [?] & handed Joe the Whiskey that they carried it in turn & left it the head of a Field in the bottom.

Tunis Hood Jr. being sworn Deposeth and sayeth, that he went into the woods where Sam was at work, where he found on his coming up Sam run but on being spoke to he returned & being further asked why he run he said there was a Horse missing last night & he was afraid that he was about to whip him for it, but on being told that was not it - was told to guess & then did say he supposed was for Whiskey for that F. Shaver lossd some last night - at same time declares he had Not said there was any missing or Whiskey stolen - Tunis Shaver & Fred: Shaver says they nor do they believe any person had told Sam of these things - Also that Joe confessed that Will a Negroe of Jno. Ford told them Viz Sam, Joe & Ben that Shaver had a Keg of Whisky & if they could take it to a certain place they could take it to a certain place they would receive it - that Sam & Joe went & did take the Whiskey & dispose of it in manner as sworn to by F. Shaver.

Alex McClure swears that he saw a Horse near to Robt. Phillips Field on Monday 21st early in the morning which said Horse he saw this day in the Possession of F. Shaver & claimed by him.

Will a Negroe fellow of Jno. Fords, being brought before us, on examination gives not any satisfactory information.

Joe a Negroe Fellow of Tunis Hood Senr. being brought also before us, declares that he was aiding and abetting in taking a Horse the property of Tunis Shaver, which Negroe Ben did ride away.

Ben a Negroe Fellow of Robt. Phillips declares that he together with Joe the aforesaid & Sam a Negroe Fellow of Ezekl. Black, did take & catch a Horse, which they agreed was Tunis Shavers, & afterwards did agree to take or steal some Whisky from Fred. Shaver & that they all went together to a rock on the creek within a small distance of Shavers House, where was Ben was left & the other two went forward to execute the design but further knows not of the Whisky.

Sam Acknowledges to the taking of the Horse but further denies.

Reuben Hood declared on oath, that after some punishment being inflicted on Joe he declared he [?] the Whisky and described a place & after going to said place he showed where but on being told it was improbable he altered & showed another - after being called aside by the said Reuben & to tell the truth, he declared that the Whisky was taken and carried to the said place.

The Jury on examination of the facts have unanimously agreed, that the aforesaid Negroes, Ben, Joe, & Sam are guilty of taking the Horse & Whisky and adjudge that they on tomorrow at the hour of two be taken to the public Whipping Post & there receive on their backs fifty lashes well laid on each, also that Robert Phillips, Tunis Hood Senr. & Ezekiel Black pay unto Frederick Shaver Four pounds ten Shillings, viz. thirty shillings each together with all costs & Charges accruing on the prosecution and conviction of the aforesaid Negroes & that the said Negroes stand confined in the custody of the Sheriff untill the costs be paid.

Signed under our hands & Seals this 25th day of April 1793.

Will: Polk owner of slaves		Hez. Alexander JP	(Seal)
Robert Wilson	ditto	John Ford JP	(Seal)
Jno McCullah	ditto	Geo Graham JP	(Seal)
C[?] Polk	ditto		

****

State Vs. a Slave [Name not given] [1774]
Criminal Action
Felony (Stealing)
Mecklenburg County

North Carolina }
Pasquotank County }

These may Certify that a Negro Man the Property of Moriam Jones Orphan of Griffeth Jones being convicted and found Guilty of Felony was valued to Eight Pounds Proclamation Money.

Given Under my hand and Seal at the Clerks office at Winfield this 15th day of August 1774
Test Thos. Macknight

[Editor's note: This slave had been executed for a felony. Under North Carolina law a slave owner was reimbursed by the State for executed slaves. This law was in effect until 1786.]

Chapter Three

Mecklenburg County

Free Persons of Color

Free Persons of Color

Saml Yontz & John Hunters Bond for
Tom Baker free Man of Color, April Term, 1858

April Term 1858
I Certify that John Walker, John P. Ross and John M Potts are the Justices presiding and approve this bond
W Reid

Know all Men by these presents that we Samuel Yontz and John Hunter are each held & firmly bound unto the State of North Carolina in the Sum of Five hundred dollars, Current Money of Said State, for the which payment Well and truly to be Made and done, We bind Ourselves and each of our heirs, administrators or assigns, jointly, firmly, Severally by these presents, Sealed with Our Seals and dated this the 30th day of April AD 1858.

Now therefore the Condition of the above Obligation is such that whereas the above bounden Samuel Yentz, has living with him Tom Baker, a free boy of Color -- Now if the Said Tom Baker shall demean himself well, during his Stay, with the said Samuel Yontz, then the above Obligation to be Void Otherwise to Remain in full force & Effect.
Signed Sealed & delivered in the presence of us
W. Reid Esq — Samuel Yontz (Seal)
John Hunter (Seal)

****

North Carolina }
Mecklinburg County }

Susan Smith & Lucretia Smith Persons of Colour (and Daughters of Susan Smith Senr. a person of Colour) having been put under the direction of their Sd. Mother by the order of this Worshipfull Court to be Raised Represent that they have both arrived at full age and pray that it be Entered on Record and a Certificate thereof Given them.

****

Bond for Plumb, a free Negro

State of North Carolina,

Know all Men by these Presents, That Hugh Torrence and John McKnitt Alexander are held and firmly bound unto Nathaniel Alexander & James Conner Esquires, and the rest of the Justices assigned to keep the peace for Mecklenburg County, in the just and full sum of three Hundred pounds, current money of the said State, to be paid to the Said Nathaniel Alexander, his heirs, executors, administrators or assigns: To the which payment well and truly to be made, we bind ourselves, and every of us, our and each of our heirs, executors, and administrators, jointly and severally, firmly by these presents. Sealed with our Seals, and dated this 28th day of October Anno Dom. 1800.

Whereas the above bounden Hugh Torrence hath been this day, by the worshipful court of said county, appointed Guardian to Plumb a free Negro. Now the condition of the above obligation is such, that if the said Hugh Torrence Guardian as aforesaid, shall well and truly discharge his said guardianship, by taking care of and improving all the estate belonging to the said orphan; and shall also settle his guardianship accounts with the court of said county, as is required by law; and that he will deliver up to the said Plumb as aforesaid, all such estate as he ought of right to be possessed of agreeable to the true intent and meaning of the act of the general Assembly in such case made and provided; then this obligation to be void, otherwise to remain in full force and virtue.

Signed, Sealed and Delivered Hugh Torrence (Seal)
in the presence of JM Alexander (Seal)

Chapter Four

Mecklenburg County

Hiring of Slaves

Wilmington, Charlotte & Rutherford Rail Road Company.

No. 22

Know all men by these presents, That on the first day of January next, the Wilmington, Charlotte & Rutherford Rail Road Company will pay to Junius A. Fox, or order, at the Office of the Treasurer of the Company, Six Hundred & seventy five dollars, for the hire of negros - Viz. for Sam $250 - Stephen $150 - Paul $150 & Jack $125 from the 1st day of Jany., 1861, to the 25th day of December, 1861, and that said Company will feed & clothe said Negroes during the said term of service, call in medical aid when necessary, and pay double value for said slaves, if lost by being carried out of the State of North Carolina by said Company, and to lose all runaway time.

In Witness Whereof, the President of said Company hath set his hand and affixed the seal of the corporation, this 1st day of January, 1861. W. Guion, President.

****

$200.00 Charlotte April 1st 1854

On the first day of January 1855 we or either of us promise to pay W.L. Hairston or Order the Sum of Two hundred Dollars the same being for Hire of two Boys named Elam & Abram for the present Year.

As witness our hands & Seals

John E. Penman (Seal)
W.W. Elms (Seal)

$250.00 Charlotte January 12th 1854

On the first day of January 1855 we or either of us promise to pay Dr. W.W. Orr the sum of Two hundred & fifty Dollars the same being for hire of two negroe men called William and King for one Year as witness our hands & seals.

John E. Penman (Seal)
W.W. Elms (Seal)

$ Charlotte Jan'y 16th 1854

Twelve months after date We or either of us promise to pay Wm. F. Davidson the sum of sixty Dollars the same being for hire of Girl Fanny for for one year from date as witness our hands & Seals.

John E. Penman (Seal)
W.W. Elms (Seal)

$1000.00 Charlotte Jany 5th 1854

Twelve months after date We or either of us promise to pay William Johnston for the hire of 5 Boys each at $200.00 -- the sum of One thousand Dollars. We are not to cloth the said Boys as witness our hands & seals

John E. Penman (Seal)

$150.00 Charlotte January 2nd 1854

Twelve months after date we or either of us promise to pay Joseph B. McDonald for hire of Boy Jack for the year 1854 the sum of One hundred and fifty Dollars as witness our hands and seals.

John E. Penman (Seal)
W. W. Elms (Seal)

$150.00 Charlotte January 2nd 1854

Twelve months after date we or either of us promise to pay G.W. McDonald for the hire of Boy Billy for the year 1854 the sum of one hundred & fifty Dollars as witness our hands and seals.

John E. Penman (Seal)
W.W. Elms (Seal)

$150.00 Charlotte January 2nd 1854

Twelve months after date we or either of us promise to pay John M. Shelby for hire of Boy Jack for the year 1854 the sum of one hundred and fifty Dollars as witness our hands and seals.
John E. Penman (Seal)
W.W. Elms (Seal)

$220.00 Charlotte March 1st 1854
On the first day of January 1855 We or either of us promise to pay W.R. Rankin the sum of two hundred and Twenty Dollars the same being for hire of one negro Boy named Abe for the present Year it is well understood that we are not to clothe the said Boy Abe, and we pay no Doctors Bill for said Boy should he be sick. As witness our hands & seals.
John E. Penman (Seal)
W.W. Elms (Seal)

Twelve months after date we or either of us promise to pay Margaret M. Davidson five hundred and seventy dollars for the hire of the negroes Stephen & Allie and Julius for twelve months.
January 2, 1854
John E. Penman (Seal)
W.W. Elms (Seal)

Twelve months After date we or Either of us promise to pay J.D. Williamson or order the sum of One Hundred & fifty Dollars for the Hire of a Boy named Alexander for 12 months this the 30th day of December 1853
$150.00
John E. Penman (Seal)
W.W. Elms (Seal)

On the first day of January next we or either of us promise to pay D.A. Caldwell Eleven hundred and thirty four dollars value secured.
Witness our hands & seals this 21st day of January 1854.
John E. Penman (Seal)
W.W. Elms (Seal)

$190.00 Charlotte January 2nd 1854

Twelve months after date We or either of us promise to pay Mrs. Susanna Baker the sum of one hundred & ninety Dollars the same being for the hire of Boy Alick for the year 1854 as witness our hands and seals.
John E. Penman (Seal)
W.W. Elms (Seal)

****

Articles of Suit
1832

Articles of the present hireing Are as follows --
1st The highest bidder will be considered the purchaser for one year

2nd The knocking down by the Cryer will be considered the delivery

3rd Persons hireing Negroes at this sale will be bound to furnish them with the following articles of Clothing (viz) two shirts, two pair of pantaloons and one vest suitable for Summer, one suit suitable fro Winter consisting of one pair of pantaloons one shirt one waistcoat and one roundabout Lincy or woole Coat a wool hat a Blankett & a pair of double soled shoes and pay the tax on said negro or negroes, the females to be clothed in like manner according to their (Sect**[?]**) the negroes so Hired to be returned to the Guardians on the twenty sixth day of December next unavoidable accidents excepted on these premises, persons hireing will be bound to give approved security for the faithful performance in furnishing Clothing as well as for the payment of the hires.
Decr. 26th 1832 Joseph Reed
Test J Smith
Hugh M. Lee

****

State of North Carolina
Mecklinburg County

This day Joseph Maxwell Came before me the subscribing Justice of the peace for sd County and made oath that William Monteeth and his brother Josiah Hired a family of negroes on the tenth of November 1896 Consisting of a man and woman and boy & girl, he also deposeth & say that Josiah Monteeth had in possession for the term of one year the woman & girl and William the Man & boy, he also sayeth he believes that they hired this sd family of negroes in partnership, he also sayeth that those negroes Hired for Eighty one or two lbs., he also sayeth that he believes that this is the note given to James [?] for sd Hire of Negroes at that time. Knowing or believing that the signature to this note to be Josiah Monteeths.

Sworn to and subscribed before me this 24th day of August 1827
Test Joseph Maxwell
J Doherty JP

****

The articles of the present hireing are as follows

1st The highest bidder will be the purchaser for the term of one year, or untill the 31st day of December next.

2nd Persons hireing at the present sale will be bound to give two approved securities & furnish the Negro or Negroes so Hired by them with the following articles of Clothing (Viz) two suits of clothes consisting of one pair of pantaloons made of good Cotten Cloth and onr shirt in each for Summer ware one suit suitable for Winter consisting of one pair of pantaloons, one shirt, one coat, the Coat and pantaloons to be at least half wool, one pair of Double soled shoes, one pair socks, a wool hat and a good blankett and return the Negro or negroes so hired to the Guardians on the premises on the 31st day of December as above stated (Death excepted)
December 31st 1828
N.B. the Females are to be Clothed in like manner according to there Sect and the hirer pays the tax on the Negroes So hired by them.
A.W. Alexander, J Smith, Jas. McCullah, Joseph Reed

****

The Articles of the present hireing and renting are as follows

1st The highest Bidder will be considered the purchaser for the term of twelve months.

2nd Any person or persons hireing negros at the present hiring will be Bound to furnish the men & Boys so hired by them with the following articles of Clothing (Viz) two pair of new pantaloons and two new shirts suitable for Summer ware, made of good strong cloth, one pair of new lincy or woolen cloth pantiloons, one waistcoat & one Coat made of good Lincy Cloth, and a new cotton shirt suitable for winter, one pair of Double Soled Shoes, pair woolen socks, a wool hat and a Blankett and pay the tax on said negro or Negroes for the present year, the Females are to be clothed in like manner according these [?] all persons hireing negroes or renting land will be Bound to give there notes with approved security to the Guardians.

Decr. 26th 1833	Joseph Reid
Test	Hugh M. Lee
	J Smith[?]

****

Negroes Hired on the 2d day of January 1838 to the 25th December of the same year (1838) as follows

Nathan Orr	Boy Cato	$30.25
Stephen D. Manson	Boy Grandison	8.01
Kindred Stewart	Boy Joe	2.25
	Girl Ester & two children	

This Boy Jo was taken from Stuart By his Mistress for bad usage therefore I am not Bound for the Hire

---

A List of Hireing for 1839 Hired on the 26th December 1838

	Negroes Names	
Levi Russ	Joseph Sen.	$41.75

Charles X Baker	Washington note	5.45
William X Biram	Joseph junr. note	1.55
Stephen Manson	Granderson note	11.00
Nathen X Oar	Cato note	21.35
Caty Hannon	Easter & two children to the lowest bidder	28.50

Negroes Hired of Dorcas McLearty, Jos Reid as Agent -- at Peoples Store Dec. 24th, 1842 - For the year 1843

Names of Negroes	Names of Purchaser	
Albert	Amos P. Alexander	1.47
note Washington	Wm. Doster	9.25
note Joe senr.	John N. Lee	12.24
note Catoe	Amos P. Alexander	7.00
Young Joe	John Weeks	6.40
Bill	W.G. Phillips	.10
Easther & Jim Taylor	Richd. Peoples	3.00
		39.68

****

Notio

I will offer at my house On the 26th day of the Present month Eight likely Negroes men, Women and Boys to be hired for the term of twelve months And also a valuable tract of land for the said time if not Rented before that time this Dec. 15, 1840

Joseph Reed, Guardian

Chapter Five

Mecklenburg County

Petition Ex Parte

Araminta Query & Margaret E. Query
Ex Parte, Petition for Division of Negroes
To April Sessions 1847

Z. Morris, A. Harrison, John Bass**[?]**, Freeholders
Wilson Atto.

North Carolina }Court of Pleas & Quarter
Mecklenburg County } Sessions April Term 1847

To the Worshipful the Justices of the Court of pleas and quarter sessions for said County

The petition of Araminta Query and Margaret E. Query an infant who by her next friend Margaret Query, all of sd. County respectfully represent to your Worships that they are seized and possessed as Tenants in Common of the following Slaves To Wit, March, Charlotte, Jacob, John and Sarah - Your petitioners further represent to your Worships that they are desirous that a division of sd. Negroes should be made between them. They therefore pray your Worships to appoint three freeholders **[?]** with your petitioners to divide said Negroes, **[Torn]** allot to each her share in severally, And your petitioners as in duty bound will ever pray.
Wilson, Atto

****

State of North Carolina } In Equity
Mecklenburg County } Fall Term 1856

Mecklenburg County

To the Honorable the Judge of the Superior Court of Law & Equity for said County.

The petitioner of June, Parks, Harrison, Lenora and Joseph McCombs, infants, under the age of twenty one years who sue by their Guardian E.C. Wallace, respectfully represent to your Honor, that they are the owners of the following Negroes, as Tenants in Common to wit, Jake aged about fifty five years, Sam aged about Ten years, Bob aged about nine years, Nancy aged about fifty five years, Leah aged about thirty years and her two children aged about two years & nine months, Henry aged about twenty two years To Wit, **[?]** being Eight in number - That sd. Negroes have to be hired out from year to year - That two of them are becoming old - That being hired out, they are not properly cared for, and that your infant petitioners have heretofore sustained heavy losses by Death among their Negroes - They would further show that as property of that kind is now high that their interests would be promoted by a sale thereof - They Therefore pray your Honor to order & Decree upon such times as to your Honor shall seem most reasonable - And your petitioners as in duty bound will ever pray.
Wilson, Sct.

Ira Parks maketh Oath that he knows the negroes set forth in the foregoing petition, and that he believes that the interests of the infants would be promoted by a sale thereof.

Sworn to before me
13th Novr. 1856
D.R. Dunlap C.M. Eq.

Ira Parks
W.R. Maxwell

In this case the Clerk & Master, from the testimony laid before him, is of opinion that it would be to the Interest of the Children to have the negroes mrentioned in the Petition sold
D.R. Dunlap C.M. Eq.

By virtue of a Decree in the Court of Equity for Mecklenburg County in the case of E.C. Wallis **[?]**, the undersigned as commissioner on the 2nd day of January 1857, proceeded to sell at publick Auction the Negro Slaves in the petition mentioned, upon a Credit of twelve Months with interest - The Slaves were purchased by the following persons at the prices appended to their names, to wit

Boy Jake To J.P. Smith for	$314.00
Boy Henry To Wm McCombs for	1175.00
Girl Nancy To R.W. McCombs	205.00
Girl Leah & her two children to A. Wallace	1110.00
Boy Sam To R.H. Laffert	700.00
Boy Bob To A.J. Wallace	595.00
	$4099.00

Every purchaser gave his Bond with Security
All of which is respectfully Submitted
May 11, 1857
E.C. Wallis Commissioner}

****

State of North Carolina } In Equity to
Mecklenburg County } Fall Term 1861

To Allen Cruse

You are hereby notified that, at the next Court of Equity to be opened and held for the County aforesaid, at the Court House in Charlotte on the 11th Monday after the 4th Monday in August 1861. I shall make a motion before the Judge holding said County for a Judgment upon a bond executed by you as principal with C. Overman & S.J. Wristers Sureties, said bond payable to me as Clerk & Master in Equity in the matter of A.J. Orr & others Exparte petition to sell Slaves for the sum of one thousand four hundred & Seventy Six dollars, with interest from 31st day of Decr. 1859.
A.C. Williamson C.M.C.

Chapter Six

Mecklenburg County

Sales of Slaves

Mary Henderson to John Robinson
Deed of Trust, August Term 1819

Mecklenburg County} August Term 1919
The execution of the Within Deed was duly proven in Open Court by Isaac S. Henderson one of the subscribing Witnesses and admitted to Record and Ordered to be Registered
Test Isaac Alexander CMC

Mecklenburg County
This deed of trust or Bill of Sale was registered in my office in Book No. 21, Page 151: this 14th of Novr. AD 1819
by Wm. Alexander Reg.

State of North Carolina
This Indenture Made this 7th day of May in the year of our Lord one thousand Eight Hundred and Seventeen between Mrs. Mary Henderson of the County of Mecklenburg and State aforesaid of the one part & the Revd. John Robinson of the County of Cabarrus and State of North Carolina of the other part Witnesseth, that the Said Mary Henderson for and in Consideration of the love and Affection which she Bears to Harriet McBryde of Newberry Viledge in the State of South Carolina and also for and in Consideration of the Sum of ten Shillings to her in hand paid by the above named John Robinson and before the Signing and delivery of these presents the Receipt whereof is hereby acknowledged has granted Bargained and Sold and by these presents doth grant, bargain, Sell and Deliver unto the said John Robinson and to his Executors or Administrators and to the Survivor or Survivors of such

Executors or Administrators a certain Negro Slave Named Esther now about 20 years of age and her two children to hold the Said negro Slaves and her future Increase to him the said John and his Executors or Administrators and to the Survivor or Survivors of Such Executors or Administrators to the uses, upon the trusts, and to and for the intent and purposes and under and Subject to the provisos and agreements herein After Mentioned Expressly and declared of and Conserning the same, that is to Say - That the said John Robinson and his Executors or Administrators or the Survivor or Survivors of them shall permit the Said Harriet McBryde to have, take, and Receive to her separate use and benefit, all the profits which may arise from the use, hire, and labor of the Said Slaves and her future Increase; And on the death of the Said Harriet McBryde, then the said trustee or his Executors or Administrators or the Survivor or Survivors of such Executors or Administrators as the Case may be Shall devide the Said Negro Slaves together with her increase Equally among the children of the Said Harriet McBryde, to have and to hold the Same to the children and to their heirs Executors Administrators and assigns forever.

In Witness whereof the Said Mary Henderson hath hereunto Let her hand and seal together with the said John Robinson the day and year first above Written.

Signed and Delivered — Mary Henderson (Seal)
In presence of — Jno. Robinson (Seal)
Isaac S. Henderson Jurat
F.B. Smart

****

State of North Carolina
Mecklenburg County

Know all men by these presents that I Leroy Springs of the County and State aforesaid for and in Consideration of the sum of Fifteen Hundred Dollars to me in hand paid by Samuel A. Harris of said County and State the receipt ehereof is hereby acknowledged have given Granted bargained and sold this day and date and do hereby give Grant bargain and sell unto the said Samuel A. Harris a Certain Molatto Boy Called George a first rate shoe and Boot maker about the age of Twenty six Years and I do hereby warrant him sound in boddy and mind and I further

warrant and defend the right and title of said negro against the lawful Claims of all persons whatsoever in Testimony whereof I have hereunto set my hand and seal this 1st July 1841.
Test. Charles E. Moss Leroy Springs

****

Mortgage
George Houston to James Houston for 6 negroes
Mecklenburg County} April Sessions 1806

The execution of the within Mortgage Deed was proven in Court & Recorded
Test - Isaac Alexander

Mecklenburg County This deed or Mortgage & **[Torn]** thereon is registered in my Office in Book No. 18, page 253 this 3d July 1806
By Wm. B. Alexander register.

Know all men by these presents that I George Houston of Mecklenburg County State of North Carolina, for and in Consideration of the sum of one hundred and twenty five dollars to me in hand paid by James Houston of sd. County of sd. State the receipt whereof I do hereby acknowledge have bargained sold delivered, and by these presents do bargain , sell and deliver unto the sd. James Houston six negroes, by name Viz. Venus, Esther, Peg, Dick, Milly, and Polly; to have and to hold the sd. bargained premises unto the sd. James Houston his hrs., admrs and assigns forever , And I the sd. George Houston for myself my exrs., admrs., & assigns. Provided nevertheless that if I the sd. George Houston my exrs., admrs., & assigns, or anyone, do and shall well and truly pay or cause to be paid unto the sd. James Houston his exrs., admrs., or assigns the sum of one hundred and twenty five dollars on the first of Jany 1808 with Lawfull interest for the same, for redemption of the sd. bargained premises then this bill of sale to be void, or else to remain in full force - in witness whereof I have hereunto set my hand & seal this 10th April 1806.
In presence of George Houston (Seal)
Wm. Morrison Jurat

****

State of No. Carolina }
Mecklenburg County }
Feb. the 28th, 1826 }

Know all men by these presents that I David Hoss for and in consideration of the sum of three hundred and twenty five dollars hath bargained and sold and by these presents do bargain and sell to Thomas J. Johnson & James H. Blake a negroe girl by the name of Nelly the right and title of which rights give I warrant and defend to the said Thomas J. Johnson and James H. Blake and their heirs forever.

The condition of the above obligation is such for that which the above bounden David Hoss hath purchased of Hesture[?] S. Kimble a negro girl for the sum of three hundred and twenty five dollars, and the said Thomas J. Johnson & James H. Blake hath bound themselves as security for the payment of the same - And if the said David Hoss shall pay the above sum of three hundred twenty five dollars to H.S. Kimble to twelve months from the date hereof then the above obligation to be void otherwise remain in full force and virtue.

The testimony whereof I have hereunto affixed my hand and seal
David Hoss (Seal)

Mecklenburg County August sessions 1826
I hereby certify that the within Mortgages was duly proven in Court by John P. Bates a Subscribing witness and Recorded
Test Isaac Alexander CMC
David Hoss, Thomas J. Johnson, James H. Blake, Mortgage

****

Delivery Bond - David Crockett

State of North Carolina
Mecklinburg County

Mecklenburg County

Know all men by these Presents that I John Mcutchin am held and firmly Bound unto David Crocket in the sum of of Three Hundred Pounds Specie to the which Payment well and truly to be made to the said David Crockett his Heirs Executors Administrators or assigns I bind myself my Heirs Executors Administrators jointly and severally firmly by these Presents sealed with my seal Dated this 15th Day of November 1785.

The Condition of the above obligation is such that if the above Bounden John Mcutchin doth Deliver to the said David Crocket a Healthy sound smart Negro not under Ten year old, nor above Twelve the said McCutchin to Deliver said Negro at or Before the Last of January in the year 1786 then this obligation shall be Void otherwise to Remain in full force and Virtue in Same.

Signed sealed and Delivered Jno. McCutchen (Seal)
in Presence of us, Francis Gordon, **[Name smeared],** William Allin.

Paid to John McCutchin £126
I Do hereby assign over my Right and Title of the within Bond to William Alexander for Value Received
David Crocket

Chapter Seven

Mecklenburg County

Coroner's Inquests

State of North Carolina }
Mecklenburg County }

James Barnett acknowledged Bound in a Recognizance to the State in the sum of Fifty Dollars to be void on condition he appears at the Court house in Charlotte and give evidence against Moses and Jacob two slaves who stand Charged with the Murder of a Slave and have been comitted to the County gaol acknowledged before me 3rd March 1808.
Jas. Tagert JP
Geo W. Smart JP

The State Vs. Slaves
Executed by Wm. Berryhill

State of North Carolina }
Mecklenburg County }

To a sworn officer to execute & return Without Delay - whereas it has been Represented to me Geo W Smartt one of the Justices for this County by Jas. Sprott Esquire that a Negro man the property of Joseph Sprot of South Carolina by name Jacob was found on this morning March 19th 1808 lying on the Road some where near to Mr Hugh McDowals in the county aforesaid from appearance - Dangerously wounded on the head his Life is Doubtfull and whereas there appears to be good grounds to believe that Capt. Hugh Parks Ephraham, Jas. McNights Moses, Jas. Sprotts, Esquires Jacob can give some information on the Subject that the whole or a part of them were at or are guilty of the perpetration of this

Crime you are therefore commanded in the name of the State to take such assistance with you as you may Deem Necessary and take the whole of the above named Negroes before some Justice of the Peace for this County to be further Delt with as from law and evidence may appear to be Necessary and this shall be your Warrant given under my hand and Seal this 19th Day of March 1808.
Geo. W. Smart JP (Seal)
The Slave Ephraim is still Liable to be taken on this Warrant.

State of N. Carolina }
Mecklenburg County }

To William Berryhill one of the Constables of the County aforesd.

We hereby command you in the name of the State to Summon twenty four Freeholders of this County to appear before us tomorrow at 12 Oclock at noon at the House of Hugh McDowel in sd. County to Execute such things as shall be given them in Charge on behalf of the State: and you are also Commanded to then and there yourself, to shew how you shall have executed this precept. Given under our hands and Seals this 19th March 1808.
Jno. Kendrick JP (Seal)
Jas. Tagert JP (Seal)

State of North Carolina }
Mecklenburg County }

Hugh McDowel being Called upon and sworn before a Jury of Inquest held at the House of sd. Hugh McDowel on the 20th March 1808 on the Dead Body of a Negro man Slave belonging to Joseph Sprott Named Jacob, Deposeth as followeth (to wit) That he the sd. Hugh McDowel on the 19th Instant early in the morning he was informed by a Negro fellow named Chance owned by Abram Taylor that there was a negro man lying on the ground between sd. McDowels fence and the Creek, on which he went to see, and found the Negro with a large Wound in his forehead almost breathless, and an axe lying about two or three feet from him.

Alexander Porter being Called on and Sworn to give evidence as aforesaid; Deposeth as follows - (to wit) that on the 19th Instant he found a hat lying in the road about two hundred yards from where the sd. Negro was found, and blood lying near the sd. hat, and the appearance of a Shuffle on the Ground at the same place and also that there was an Iron wedge lying at the same place.

The Jury now being on the Ground where the Blood, hatt and Wedge was found, and Examined the following Negroes, after giving the necessary Charge to them to declare the truth - Chance, a Negroe fellow owned by Abram Taylor Relates, that he does not know any thing concerning how the sd. negroe came by his Death.

Jacob, a fellow belonging to James Sprott, after being Charged as aforesd., Relates that he and the now Dec'd Negro came together from James Barnetts on the evening of the 18th Instant on their way home, untill they crossed the Creek near to Hugh McDowels, where they were met by two negroe fellows one named Ephraim, belonging to Hugh Parks, and the other Named Moses, belonging to James McNight where he and sd. Ephraim, ingaged in a fight, and after fighting some time sd. Ephraim Ran, and he pursued him across the Creek and then Returned and found the now Dec'd Negro Sitting by the Root of a tree and said he was hurt, he asked what hurt him, he answered he had went against a tree; but he got up, and went with him to the Road leading to Hugh McDowels, and there he left him.

Examination of Ephraim, belonging to Hugh Parks who says, that he, and James Sprotts fellow Jacob, having had some Difference at James Barnetts on the 18th Instant, and not having liberty to fight there, he went on before and met him at the place where the hay &c were found in company with James McNights Moses, with an intention to make it up with him, or fight, at which place they ingaged and fought, and at length loosing himself from sd. Jacob he ran across the Creek pursued by Jacob James Sprotts fellow and the Negroe that is now dead, James McNights Moses being gone away - After he was over the Creek he heard a moaning on the side from which he came as of some person in great Distress, but knows not who it was, or what was the cause and that he had left his hat behind him.

Taken before us at the House of Hugh McDowels in the County aforesaid this 20th March 1808.
Jno Kendrick JP
Jas. Tagert JP

Examination of Sundry persons Concerning the Death of Jacob.

State of North Carolina
Mecklenburg County

Inquisition indented taken at the dwelling house of Hugh McDowell in the County aforesaid the 20th day of March in the year 1808 before us John Kindreck and James Tagert two of the Justices of the peace for said County upon view of the body of Jacob a Slave the property of Joseph Sprott, then and there lying dead and upon the Oath of Daniel Smith, John Porter, Wm. Todd, John Berryhill, Samuel Berryhill, John Hepworth, John Taylor, Abraham Taylor, William Campbell, Joseph Wilson, John Cathcart and John Barnett &c good and lawful men of the County aforesaid, who being charged and sworn to enquire how and in what manner the said Slave by his Death came upon their Oaths do say that on the 19th of this Instant the said Slave was found near the house of the said McDowell with a large wound in his forehead which they suppose either to be done with an Ax or an Iron wedge and that he came to his death in a violent way but cannot tell by whome from all the evidence they could get. In Testimony whereof as well we the said Justices and Jurors aforesaid to this inquisition have Severally put our hands and seals the day year and place first above mentioned.
Jas. Tagert JP
Jno. Kendrick JP

Daniel Smith	(Seal)	John Barnett	(Seal)
John Porter	(Seal)	Wm. M. Todd	(Seal)
Jno. Berryhill	(Seal)	Joseph Wilson	(Seal)
Samuel Berryhill	(Seal)	John Cathcart	(Seal)
John Hepworth	(Seal)	W. Campbell	(Seal)
Abm. Taylor	(Seal)	John Taylor	(Seal)

State of North Carolina }
Mecklinburg County }

The evidence of Negro Moses the property of Jas McNights taken before a jury of Inquest on the 31 Day of March 1808 Concerning a negro Slave Jacob the property of Joseph Sprott found near to Mr. Hugh McDowalls

on the morning of the 19th Inst. badly wounded of which wound he Died this Moses Saieth on the night before said Jacob was found that Capt. Parks Ephraham and Jas Sprotts Jacob Differed at the house of Jas Barnetts Mr. Barnett would not allow them to fight that some time after he this said Moses and Ephram turned and went down the Creek that Ephram said he would go and fight or make it up that after they got over the Creek they stopped until the two Jacobs Came up, Ephram asked Who are you and Jas Sprots Jacob Replied what are you doing there, Ephram says a man and I want to know if you are the same man you were at the house, they got together and fought and while fighting Joseph Sprotts Jacob struck Ephram and further saieth that Joseph Sprotts Jacob struck him the said Moses with an Ax and then he said Moses Run off and Ephraim Cleared himself Likewise
Jas. Tagert JP
Geo W. Smart JP

State of North Carolina }
Mecklenburg County }

The evidence of Jas. Barnet taken before a Jury of Inquest held on the body of a Negro by the name of Jacob the property of Joseph Sprot that was found lying on the Road near to Hugh McDowels Dangerously Wounded on the morning of the 19 of March 1808 in the County of Mecklinburg this Deponent Saith that on Fryday evening March 19 at this Deponents house a Quarell began between Jas. Sprotts Jacob & Capt. Hugh Parks Epharam and a scuffle ensued that he this Deponant parted them and ordered them home, this Deponant told said Negro of Capt Parks of Did not go home he Would tell his Master, the Negro Epharam Swore that he Did not care for him or his Master Either and that he would which Jas. Sprotts Jacob this he Swore more than once, Some time after on the same night this Deponant saieth that he heard quareling Down the Creek and Started to go but before he got there it ceased but heard some person say Dam you what brought you here.

Taken at the house of Jas. McNights on the 31 day of March 1808.

Sworn to before us James Barnett
Jas Tagert JP
Geo W. Smart JP

State of North Carolina }
Mecklenburg County }

To the Sheriff or Keeper of the common gaol of said County

These are to command you in the name of the State to Receive into your Goal the Bodys of Moses a Slave the property of James McKnight and Jacob the property of Jas. Sprott Esqr. who are on strong presumption charged with the Murder of Jacob a Slave the property of Joseph Sprott and them safely keep in your said Gaol and custody until they be thence discharged by one course of law.

Given under our hands and Seals at office the 31st of March 1808
Jas. Tagert JP (Seal)
Geo. W. Smart JP

State of North Carolina }
Mecklenburg County }

To the Sheriff of Mecklenburg County, Greeting:

You are hereby commanded to Summon Isaac Mason personally to be and appear before the Justices of the County Court of Pleas and Quarter Sessions to be held for the County of Mecklenburg at the court house in Charlotte on the fourth Monday of April Instant next; then and there to testify and the truth to say in behalf of the State in a certain matter of controversy before said court depending, and then and there to be tried; wherein the State is plaintiff, and Ephraim, Moses & Jacob is defendents. And this you shall in no wise omit under the penalty by lae enjoined.

Witness Isaac Alexander Clerk of our said court, at Charlotte the 4th Monday of April 1808 and in the XXXII year of our independence.
Isaac Alexander Clk

State of North Carolina }
Mecklenburg County }

To the Sheriff of Mecklinburg County, Greeting:

You are hereby commanded to Summon Hugh McDowel personally to be and appear before the Justices of the County Court of Pleas and Quarter Sessions to be held for the county of Mecklenburg at the court house in Charlotte on the fourth Monday of April Instant next; then and there to testify and the truth to say in behalf of the State in a certain matter of controversy before said court depending, and then and there to be tried; wherein the State is plaintiff, and Ephraim, Moses & Jacob is defendant. And this you shall in no wise omit under the penalty by law enjoined.

Witness Isaac Alexander Clerk of our said court, at Charlotte the 4th Monday of April 1808 and in the XXXII year of our independence.
Isaac Alexander Clk.

State of North Carolina }
Mecklenburg County }

Inquisition indented taken at the dwelling house of James M Night in the County aforesaid the 31st day of March 1808 before us George W. Smart and James Tagert two of the Justices of the Peace for the said County upon the view of the Body of Jacob a Slave the Property of Joseph Sprott at his deceas in possession of Thomas Sprott whom thay had all seen lying dead and upon the Oath of Daniel Smith, John Porter, William Todd, John Berryhill, Samuel Berryhill, John Hepworth, John Taylor, William Campbell, Joseph Wilson, John Cathcart, John Barnett and William Porter, &c good and lawful men of the County aforesaid Who Being charged and Sworn to enquire how and in what manner the said Slave by his death came who was found lying near the Dwelling of Hugh McDowell on the 19th of this Instant early in the morning alive with a large wound in his forehead of nearly two inches square supposed to be done either with the **[Torn]** of an Ax or an Iron Wedge he could not speak when found and died that day and the Jury on their Oaths do say they think he came by his Death in a Violent way and the Jury do say that they have strong presumption to believe from the evidence they have got that Moses a slave the property of Jas. M Night and Ephraim the property of Hugh Parks and Jacob the property of Jas. Sprott Esqr. perpetrated the said crime and the strongest presumption is that it was either Ephraim or Moses in testimony whereof we the said Justices as well as the Jurors to

this inquisition have severall put our hand and seal the day year and place first above mentioned.
Jas. Tagert JP, Geo. Smart JP

Jno. Barnet	(Seal)	Samuel B'Hill	(Seal)
Daniel Smith	(Seal)	Jno Berryhill	(Seal)
W. Campbell	(Seal)	Joseph Wilson	(Seal)
John Cathcart	(Seal)	John Hepworth	(Seal)
John Porter	(Seal)	John Taylor	(Seal)
William Porter	(Seal)	Wm. M. Todd	(Seal)

North Carolina }
Mecklinburg County }

To the Sheriff or Jailor of said County

I send you herewith the body of Ephraim (a Slave) belonging to Capt. H. Parks taken by Hue & Cry upon Warrant of Jas. Tagert Esqr. a Justice of the Peace of sd. County, & brought before me by M. Bryan, Constable; the said Ephraim having been charged by the Inquisition of a Jury for Murdering a Slave the property of Joseph Sprott. These are therefore in the Name of the State to command you to receive the said Ephraim into your Jail, and him safely keep until thence discharged by due course of law.
Given under my hand & Seal this 23rd day of April 1808.
Guy Maxwell JP (Seal)

****

State of No. Carolina }
Mecklinburg County }

Inquisition indented taken at the House of the Rvd. Jas. Wallace in the County affore said on the 24th day of September in the yeare of Our Lord 1803 Before me John Patterson Coroner of the Said County upon view of the body of a Negro Child then and there lying dead And upon the Oath of Mary Parks, Poly Ray & Nancy Robinson good and Lawfull women of the County Afforesaid - Upon [?] A Negro Wench Naimed Darcus the property of Mr. Jas. Wallace And upon the Oath of Mrs. Wallace who

being Charged and sworn to Enquire how and in what Manner the sd. Negro Child came by death, came, sd. Mrs. Wallace upon hir Oath sayeth that on the 23d day of September in the yeare of our Lord 1803 did know sd. Negro Child to be found by the Rvd. Mr. Brown in A lane by Mr. Wallaces House, The Other women on their Oaths saith that finding the sd. wench Darcus in such circumstances as warrant a suspicion of being the Mother of the Child - Verdict} of the Jury --
It is the unanimous opinion of the Jury that the Corps which we have viewed is the Corps of a Negro Child which came to its death by being exposed Naked in the woods immediately After its birth that its Mother Occassioned its death and we have strong reasons to suspect Dorcus slave to Mr. Wallace to be the Mother of sd. Negro Child in testimony whereof as well & the sd. Coroner as the Jurors Aforesaid to this Inquisition have severly put our seals the day yeare and place first above Mentioned.

Willm. Mathews	(Seal)	David Rea	(Seal)
John Stephenson	(Seal)	Wm Morrison	(Seal)
Wm Stuart	(Seal)	Thos Downs	(Seal)
Jno. Patterson, Coroner		J. Robinson	(Seal)
Fridrick Aronds	(Seal)	Andw. Spratt	(Seal)
[?] McKibben	(Seal)	Samuel Downs	(Seal)
John Stitt	(Seal)		

State of North Carolina }
Mecklenburg County }

Be it remembered that on the 19th day of October 1803 Personally came before me John Patterson Coroner of the County Aforesaid Polly Parks, Polly Rea, & Nancy Robinson, All of the County Aforesaid and Acknowledged themselves indebted to the State, Viz, Each in the Sum of One hundred pounds to be Levied of each of their Goods and Chattels, Lands and tenements if default is made in the preformance of the Condition hereunder Written.

The condition of the Above recognizance is such that if the Above bounden, Polly Parks, Polly Ray & Nancy Robinson shall personally Appear before the Judges of the County Court of Law to be held for the County of Macklinburg At the Court House in Charlotte on the Twenty

Nineth day of Octr. Inst., then and there to give evidence in behalf of the State Concerning the Murder of a Negro Child wherewith Darkus Slave to the Rvd. Jas. Wallace, stands charged by an inquest taken before me upon view of the dead body of the Said Negro Child And do Not depart the said Court without leave then the Above recognizance to be Null and Void otherwise to remain in full force and Virtue.
Acknowledged before me
Jno. Patterson -- Cor

Chapter Eight

Mecklenburg County

Sheriff's Vouchers

A List of Sundry Vouchers in the Settlement of Public Acct with Tho Harris Esqr former Sheriff for the Year.

Thomas Harris Shff for the year 1774 an amount of the money in hand and a list of Vouchers as will appear By these nombers.

Cash as pr Paper **[Marked through]**

Na	L	S	d
1 Cash as pr Paper	11	0	8
2 as pr ditto	42	12	8
3 as pr do.	27	2	0
4 Hezk. Alexander	10	2	0
5 Hezk. Alexander	10	17	6
6 James Staford	3	10	6
7 Mathew Stewart	2	0	6
8 Henry Stewart	2	2	6
9 Hezk. Alexander	5	2	6
10 **[Faded]**			
11 Chas Harris	1	4	0
12 Saml. Martin	10	7	6
13 Chas Fisher	1	3	2
14 Joseph Nielson	7	3	2
15 Thos. Polk	10	3	2
16 Andrw. Gower**[?]**	1	3	2
17 G**[Faded]** Wiley	1	10	2
18 Walter Davis	1	2	6

19 as pr Certificate		10	
20 Robrt. Waker**[Walker]**	1	9	
21 Robrt. Irwin	1	10	8
22 John Caruthers		10	
23 Zachias Wilson		2	6
24 John Kilach**[?]**	10		

Years 1777, 1779 & 1778

No. Numbrs as pr Voucher	L	S	d
1 Thomas Rea	6	10	
2 Adam Alexander	10	10	
3 Willm. Moor	11	10	
4 Adam Alexander	5	4	8
5 Willm. Wiley	8		
6 Edwd. Ruth**[?]**	30	15	
7 John Wiley	5		
8 John Hood	7		
9 Hugh Forsyth	15	5	
10 John McCaul	7	4	
11 Willm. Ramsey	7	10	
12 Thos. Harris	40		
13 Thos. Black	3	8	
14 John McFa**[?]**	19	6	
15 John Davison	2	4	
16 Thos. Gibbin	34	12	
17 Aaron Alexander	5		
18 John Davis	31	8	
19 James Nicles	5	4	
20 James Alexander	3	4	
21 David Wilson	3	4	
22 John MacKnit Alexander	3	4	
23 Francis Beadly	1	4	
24 James Harris	28.6	14	10
25 Ephram Alexander	2	6	
26 John McKnit Alexander	2		
27 Robrt. Wilson	9	18	
28 James Wilson	5	1	6
29 Robrt. Wilson	7	16	

30 Thos. Harris	53	1	
31 Else Canade	16	10	
32 Martin Rods	12		
33 John Nest	3.1	6	
34 Thos. Harris	3.7	12	
35 Saml. Wilson	8	8	
36 Willm. Henderson	6	18	
37 Henry Neil	10	8	
38 John Brownfield	4	16	
39 Saml. Roage**[?]**	5		
40 Moses Thompson	8		
41 John Price	10		
42 James Berry	7	4	
43 Elizabeth Berry	3	2	
44 Walter Davis	6		
45 Robert McLeary	3	5	
46Thos. Ferguson	47	6	
47 Saml Blackwood	4	8	
48 Anne Knox	4	0	
49 John Garrison Examine this allowed	5.7		4
50 Willm. Barnet	8	14	
51 Robert Barnet	11	4	
52 James Berry	20		
53 Thos. Neil **[Nickle?]**	18		
54 John Davis	0.5		
55 Richard Robinson	48	13	6
56 Richard Brown	25	19	6
57 David Johnston	32	12	
58 Henery Long	10	2	6
59 George Goodman	26	5	
60 Willm. Alexander	122	1	6
61 Andrw. Alexander	59	14	
62 Willm. Garner	61	11	
63 Christian Abinshin**[?]**	8	12	
64 Thos. Harris	120		
65 Andrw. McCombs	0.2	16	
66 John Harris examine this			

allowed	327	17	
67 Saml. Wilson	4	10	
68 Thomas McCorkle	39	8	
69 Edwd. Gibins	29	12	
70 Willm. Alexander	2		
71 James Rice	4	8	
72 George Cathey **[Marked through]**			
73 David Sloan	5		
74 James Wilson	8	8	
75 Willm. Wilson	73	1	
76 Joseph Gilasbe	4	16	
77 Willm. Alexander	2	6	
78 Robert Pots	10		
79 Archibald Ramsey	5	12	
80 Feals Barager	19	12	
81 Willm. Alexander	64	12	6
82 Henry Monteith	3		
83 John Cathey	8		
84 Michael Henderson	3		
85 John Duckworth	3	14	
86 Ezekiel Alexander	7	4	
87 Fields Briga	10	5	
88 Saml. Stanford			
89 Hugh McQueen	6	10	
90 Matthias Berringer	21	8	
91 Michael Fisher	11	12	
92 David Spack	18	12	
93 James Alexander	12		
94 Willm. Alexander	12		
95 Agnes Allan	5		
96 George Couzine	2	8	
97 Caleb Fifer	3		
98 John March	2	10	
99 Joseph Rogers	4	8	
100 Robert Martin	18	8	
101 Hugh McRee	137		
102 Charles Reece	14	8	
103 John Armstrong	3	10	

104 James Mac_ ole	2	10	
105 Christian Barnhardt	22	16	
106 John Holebrook	24	2	
107 Hugh Paterson	23	16	
108 Saml. Patten	4	8	8
109 Saml. Paterson	1	10	
110 Willm. Huston	83	12	
111 Hans Justus	4		
112 Ezekias Wilson	9	4	
113 Charles Townsend	19	12	
114 Saml. Kellie	34	8	
115 Willm. Wilson	16	15	
116 Thos. Harris	72	16	
117 John Johnston	2	19	
118 John Johnston	8		
119 Saml. Flanekin	56	6	
120 Hugh McLellan	29	13	
121 Andra Rea	12		
122 Henery McWhorter	3	8	
123 James Shanks	13	4	
124 Andrew Neil	8	8	
125 Hugh McLellan	19	16	
126 James Johnston	4	10	
127 Gordon Potter	1	12	
128 Mary Diarman	4	10	
129 Henery Downs	12		
130 Mary Star	26		
131 Hugh Barnet	12	12	
132 John Johnston	15	6	3
133 Saml. Flanekin	27	12	
134 James Weatherspoon	15		
135 Willm. Mathews	12	16	6
136 Sarah Nisbet	20		
137 Abraham Millar	27	10	
138 John Weatherspoon	9		
139 Willm. Pigine	7		
140 James M. Callie	26	15	
141 Thomas Harris	3		
142 Joseph Downs	14	12	6

143 Joseph Moor	11	18	
144 George Callie	31	2	6
145 James Canade	2	16	
146 Willm. Clark	2	16	
147 Elisabeth Davis	20		
148 John Carson	2	12	
149 John Tool	8	8	
150 John Hair	3		
151 Robrt. McKnight	8	8	
152 Isaac Williams	26	13	6
153 James Jack Examin allowed	29	13	6
154 John McRee	19		
155 James Reed	2		
156 George Nicolson		16	
157 Joseph Graham	6		
158 John McRee Examin allowed	163	6	
159 James Harris	366	4	
160 John Hunter	11	8	
161 John McLure	3	8	
162 George Baker	3	12	
163 James Wilson	14	17	
164 John McRee	5	8	
165 Joseph Graham	11	9	
166 Elias Canade	32	6	
167 Nathaniel Monteith	2	6	
168 Berty McKay	3		
169 Joseph Moor	3	10	
170 James Wason	14	17	
171 James Canon	4	4	
172 Robrt. Henderson	8		
173 Nathaniel Smith	48	10	
174 Michael Shaver	3	12	
175 Willm. McCullich	11	14	
176 John Garrison	4	16	
177 Mathew Mc Luer	2	10	
178 James Thompson	47	6	
179 John Sharp	8		
180 James Canon	5		
181 James Thompson	5	12	

182 Andrw. McLerey	95	14
183 Robrt. Karr	2	
184 Joseph Karr	1	
185 Gidion Thompson	21	8
186 James Beadly	8	
187 David Russle	1	10
188 Conrod Hess	6	5
189 Saml. White	1	9
190 James Harris	3	12
191 Robrt. Anderson	4	
192 George Farr	10	
193 George Farr	12	
194 Daniel Davis	6	12
195 Daniel Davis	6	12
196 James Barr	4	
197 Robrt. Harris	2	15
198 John Gilpatrick	1	9
199 Anne Paterson	14	5
200 John Hamilton	9	
201 James Benson	2	8
202 John Currey	9	
203 Matthew Moffet	55	4
204 John Mcrae	2	8
205 Archibald Huston	1	1
206 Jacob Morton	18	10
207 Thos. Shields		16
208 Willm. Shields	2	
209 Saml. Brown	11	4
210 Margaret Farr	3	8
211 Efram Farr	8	10
212 Charles Reece	2	16
213 Elisabeth Farr	21	
214 [?] Alexander	4	8
215 David Bradford	3	18
216 Isaac Sanford	4	16
217 Reece Price	6	10
218 Christian Goodman	32	
219 Michael Goodman	10	

220 Philip Wolf	20		
221 Michael Goodman	10	4	
222 Thondukeo	20		
223 James Alexander	60		
224 Lynard Stands	8		
225 Philip Haffley	10		
226 Tobias Goodman	17	8	
227Niclos Creece	6	5	
228 John Jonston	9		
229 Pettar Bugar	47	5	
230 Jacob Perry	24	10	
231 George Clans	11	17	
232 George Files	1	12	
233 Widow Orey	9		
234 Pisle Pocktail	16		
235 Henery Huston	8	7	
236 Karnes Henderson	6	16	
237 Nathan Orr	4	7	
238 Gordon Potter	15		
239 Willm. Hoxet	2		
240 Benjamin Alexander	19		
241 Ezekiel Alexander	18	12	
242 Andrw. Robinson	15	10	
243 Willm. Hoxet	2	8	
244 Willm. Hoxet	4		
245 Willm. Hoxet	14		
246 David Parks	4	18	2
247 Robrt. Robinson	4	19	
248 James Alexander	3	12	
249 Esekia Alexander	3	15	
250 Esekia Alexander	20		
251 Mary Clark	7	10	
252 John Baird	8	12	
253 Willm. Haggens	61	14	
254 Thos. Harris	120		
255 John McKnit Alexander	59	4	
256 George Cathey examin allowed	94	7	10
257 Robrt. Scot	7	4	

258 George Davis	3		
259 Ephraim McLean	29	12	
260 James Draffin	4	4	
261 as Pr. Voucher	72	16	
262 Willm. Robinson	1	12	
263 Willm. Curtny	4	4	
264 John Hagins	20		
265 Jacob Gray	24	6	
266 John Gordon	1	4	
267 John Hugh	13	8	
268 Willm. King	15		
269 James Reece examine allowed	183		
270 as Pr. Voucher	17	4	
271 Thomas Harris	120		
272 Thos. Harris	40		
273 Mathew Stuart **[Marked Through]**			
274 Thos. Harris examine allowed	10		
275 Thos. Harris	1		
276 Major Fifer	598	14	
277 Willm. Orr	17		
278 Arthur Star	24		
279 Charles Alexander	12	10	
280 John Sample	101	10	
281 John Mcknit Alexander	125		

[Transcriber's note: The numbers from this point on begin with 232 instead of 282. There is no break in the page. Maybe the Sheriff was addled.]

232 James Hutchison	23	18	9
233 Jeremiah Clans	26	7	
234 as per Voucher	19		
235 Francis Seals	4		
236 Chonrad Shaver	3	15	
237 George Sawyer	9		
238 Jacob Miller	35	6	
239 Frederick Blyler	7		
240 Adam Walker	30		

241 Daniel Jarret	51	8	
242 George Kerher	39	4	
243 John Walker[?]	2	1	
244 Andrew Kerher	15		
245 George Fisher	15	7	6
246 Peter Quelman	27	10	
247 Martin Harkee	11		
248 Widow Hagler	7	10	
249 Melcar Foagleman	11	10	
250 John Barringer	13	12	
251 Godfred Like **[Sike?]**	13	12	
252 John Ashley	17		
253 Mathias Baringer	12		
254 Jacob Shovener	33	16	
255 Peter Seger **[Leger?]**	3		
256 Peter Heyler	17	5[?]	
257 Michael Mire	2		
258 George Wilkam	9		
259 Jacob Moirs	13	10	
260 Andrew Vance	26	15	
261 Paul Barringer	19	12	
262 George Heartsin	15		
263 William He_d[?]	22		
	484	13	6
Page 1 brought over	724		
Page 2 do	1430	13	4
Page 3 do	877	5	2
Page 4 do	934	15	9
Page 5 do	504	2	
Page 6 do	492	7	
Page 7 do	1905	1	4
	7358	5	1

Chapter Nine

Mecklenburg County

Miscellaneous Records

Miscellaneous Records
Lands Sold for Taxes

September the 6th A.D. 1847
The Following is a List of Lands which I propose to sell for the taxes due on the Different tracts, Tax for 1846, By, W.D. Humphrey, Shff

Persons Names	Acres	Valuations	$	Cts
Rebecca Screws unlisted	400	200	1	28
Silas Baisden	308	150		48
Daniel [?]	800	500		60
John Carter	220	100	2	32
Daniel Futeral	187	150	1	48
Lemuel Williams	20	20		6½
Stephen Brock	122	75		24
William Aman	130	130		41
Britton Dawson	57	100		32
Morris Foy	396	99		32
Henry [?]	199	420	2	34
Sol. E. Grant	75	300	2	96
John Ketchum	400	200	1	64
Barnabas Lasy	100	50	1	16
Aretus Melton	120	300	1	96
Ruthy Petteway	50	50		16
William Street	3353	1500	5	80
John Walters Sr.	493	650	4	08

David Williams	100	50		16
David Da[?]ley not listed	100	175	1	12
Isaac Watts Do.	50	25		16
Hughes & Barnam Do.	50	50		32
Daniel [?] Do.	50	50		32
Mary Arnold	50	50		16
John Bloodgood	200	200		64
Robert Caston	750	150	1	48
Daniel Heady	109	600	2	92
Hezakiah Jones	50	50		16
William Melton	150	150	1	48
Charlott Owens	75	80		25
Henry Odham	334	335	2	13
Thomas Riggs	150	90	1	28
Elijah Smith	130	75		24
Robert Caston	150	150	1	48
Meltial Morton	160	175	1	48
Levi Tilman	70	75	1	24
Polly Bearden not listed	100	100		64
Benj Jenkins	100	100	4	32
John Milles	100	140	1	44
Berry Parker	150	150	1	48
Turner Ellis Sr.	50	300	2	96
John Parker	240	240	2	76
William Collins	130	195		62
Elisha Eubanks	75	112½		36
John S. Jones[?]	300	2700	12	64
Brice Morris	70	70		22
Peter C. Morton	465	1162½	6	72
E.M. Olliver	31	62	1	19
Marian Newbold	68	204		65
Erasmus Olliver	50	75	1	24
William Parker Sr.	60	125	2	38
Asa Rigs	379	370	1	18
James M. Scott	805	2012½	9	44
Robert Whorton	100	300	1	96
Elizabeth Barber	360	500	2	60
Joseph M. French	500	500	8	60

Abram M. Hewitt	630	500	6	60
Parnal D. Marshall	225	325	3	04
Allen B. Jones Sr.	50	5	1	1½
William Melton	150	150	1	48
Thomas Owens	25	10	1	03
David W. Scott	433	383	3	22
Eli W. Stephens	240	250	1	80
Bryan Walls	6	10	1	03
Allen Phillipps	200	50	1	16
Betsey Venters unlisted	83	100		64
John Errixon	252	200		64
Micajah Paseur[?]	100	100	1	32
John Smith	154	300	1	96
Suny Wilson	50	100		32
Hope Lawrence	100	100		32
Daniel Cary	125	375	1	20
John [?]	100	150	2	48
Thomas Littleton	300	50	1	16
Henry Crag	100	100	1	32
Richard Collins	125	400	2	28
Robert Carney	50	100	1	32
Elizabeth Humphrey	50	100		64
Elroy Littleton	100	100	1	32
Isaac Melton	335	335	2	07
Isaac Williams	190	190	3	60
Seny Mashborn	60	60	2	19

A List of Lands to Be sold for taxes
Continued tax of 1846

Benjamin Barrow	--	--	--	--
Heiros[?] New Kiver	30	180	1	14
Thomas A. Craft	100	375	2	20
Peter C. Boon	150	350	2	12
Elisha Boon	150	350	2	12
Thomas Capps	50	75	1	24
Richard Gurganus	34¼	70	1	22

Jesse Gurganus	130	130	1	41
Jonas Johnson	194	500	1	60
Frederick King	53	25	1	08
Elijah King	100	64	1	20

Septr. Term 1847 Returned in open Court
By W.D. Humphrey Shff

Shepherd Parker	50	50	1	16
Frederick Shepherd	50	50	1	16
Jacob Shepherd	150	150	1	48
Edward Ward		300	1	96

Abstract of Taxes for 1846
Districts

Stump Sound: Acres-36366, Value-55497, Lots-None, WP-73, BP-95, 1H-2, $-3.60, $-349, 4-18¾.

Lower South West: Acres-26887, Value-49243, WP-69, BP-89, 1H-None, $-None, $-315, 4-57½.

Upper South West: Acres-29008½, Value-37103, WP-67, BP-85, 1H-None, $-None, $-270, 4-73¼.

Lower Rich Lands: Acres-28206, Value-55983, WP-38, BP-156, 1H-None, $-None, $-373, 4-14¾.

Upper Rich Lands: Acres-26958, Value-59928, WP-47, BP-173, 1H-None, $-None, $-411, 4-77.

Half Moon: Acres-41892, Value-87726, Lots-9, Val-7200, WP-70, BP-282, 1H-None, $-None, $-655, 4-75¼.

North East: Acres-16455, Value-24106½, WP-50, BP-68, 1H-None, $-None, $-195, 4-14.

Wolf Pit: Acres-10008½, Value-25173¼, WP-40, BP-59, 1H-None, $-None, $-179, 4-55¼.

White Oak: Acres-23755, Value-57177, Lots-3, Val-800, WP-34, BP-146, 1H-None, $-None, $-365, 4-52½.

Not Named: Acres-14070, Value-14070, BP-23, 1h-None, $-None, $-68, 4-02.

Swans Borough: Acres-25429, Value-46053, Lots-20, Val-5660, WP-54, BP-97, 1H-None, $-None, $-316, 4-44¾.

Total Acres-279029, TotalValue-512059¾, Total Lots-32, Total Val-13650, Total WP-542, Total BP-1270, Total $-316, Total 4-85.

****

Dr. State of North Carolina in Account with Jams. Coor.

For sending an express to Cartrett County	2.5.0
For benches for the Genl Assembly Etc.	5.0.0
Commissions on the opposite Creditt	2.19.4
[?] Certificates & 4 gurie paper	5.8.0
For the use of a Room for Auditors 2 years	10.0.0
For Locks for **[Faded]**	1.10.[?]
No. 1 pd. Mckellus[?] for Canvas etc.	6.0.7
2 pd. Mr. Comsan for covers to Skylights	3.16.0
3 pd. Benjamin Egglestons Acct for work	18.14.0
For my Attendance as Auditor from May 1784 to this day	
Occassionally for which I charge 78 days 24/pd.	93.12.0
Feby 1785	
	149.12.11
Cr.	
By amount of money recd for out houses Sold at the Palace	
in July 1784 & Vendue Masters Acct. herewith	59.7.1
By Ballance of this Acct. due	90.0. [?]
	149.12.11

1785 Do. State to James Coor d.3
Feby to the above Ballance 90.5.11

New Bern 15th February 1785 Errors Excepted James Coor
New Bern Feby 7th 1785
Sworn to before me
Joseph Such[?] J.P.

****

November 18th, 1803 then Received from Joab Alexander 4/ being the taxes for a Negro Wench in the possession of William Alexander for the year 1799 also received from him the sum of 7/ being the tax for two years on a Wench in the possession of Charles Wright Viz
1799 and 1800
James Neel

****

State of North Carolina
Mecklenburg County

A Return of Strays - Made by the Subscribers at February Term 1821

May the 3d 1819 Entered by Ely McCorkle living on the Waxhaw Creek a stray heffer one year to red and white with Black spots Marked on underbit out of Each Eare & Swallowfork in the Right Eare appraised to five Dollars
N.B. Bond Returned fees paid 45 cents.

July 3d 1819 Entered by Henry Meneclay[?] living on the waters of Six Mile Creek a Small sorrel Mare with a Whiteish Main and tail about thirteen hands high Eight or Nine years old No brands to be Discovered appraised to twenty five Dollars Bond Returned
Fees paid $2.20

Mecklenburg County

August the 7th 1819 Entered by James Jones living on the Waters of Twelve Mile Creek a Bay Horse about ten years Old a star in his forehead half of his Right forefoot white had on about a Dollar Bill fourteen hands high appraised to fifty Dollars, Bond Returned
fees paid $2.20

May the 12th 1819 Entered by Joseph Reid Living on the Waters of [?] mile Creek two stray sheep one [?] Marked with a Swallow fork in the Left Eare and a [?] out of the upperside of the Right Eare ... one Ram unmarked appraised to three Dollars.
N.B. Publick Money Paid $1.74.

September the 6th 1819 Entered by Matthew McCollom Living on the Waters of McCalpons Creek a year old steen white with Black spots Marked with a Cross of the Left Eare and a split in the Right Eare appraised to five Dollars
N.B. Publick Money Paid $2.87

November the 27th 1819 Entered by Samuel Johnston Cpt. ... Living on the Waters of Reid Creek a white Barrow two years old Marked with a Cross of the Left Eare and a hapenny out of the underside of the same and a Swallowfork in the Right Eare appraised to Six Dollars and fifty cents.
N.B. Publick Mony paid $4.07.

January the 6th Entered by James Ormond Living on the Waters of McCalpins Creek Neare to Harrisburg Nine head of stray Hoggs Viz their Black [?] Barrows two years old marked with a Cross of Eatch Eare and a split in the Right on Blue sow the same age Marked a Cross of Eatch Eare and a split Left eare and two slits in the Right Eare ... one old sow and foure sucking pigs the sow is Marked with a cross and two splits in Eatch Eare she is Black spoted the pigs unmarked they are appraised to Nineteen Dollars and fifty Cents.
N.B. Publick Money Paid $11.67
After the fees and Reward taken out.

February the 1st 1820 Entered by David Karr Col. Living on the Waters of Cleere Creek four head of sheep tw marked to cross two under bits in the Right Eares on with an underbit in Each Eare ... one with a Cross in the

Left Eare and a half Crop in the Right appraised to foure Dollars the whole.
N B Publick Money Paid $2.14.

February the 5th 1820 Entered by James Simpson Living on the Waters of Crookward Creek a Barrow Red with Black spots one year old Marked with a Cross of the Left Eare and a slit and a under bit in the Right Eare appraised to one Dollar fifty cents.
Returned at February Term 1821
Philemon Morris CK

****

Inventory of Negroes, Jonathan Orr

Inventory of the Negroes
Prince, 65 years old. Milly, 56 years, Serah, 55 years, Daphne, 40 years, Nancy, 28 years, Juno, 21 years, Harriet, 14 years, Doll, 5 years, Hannah, 7 years, Charlotte, 5 years, Poll, 7 years, Fanny, 6 years, Romulus, 1 year, Abpleus, 8 months, Belfast, 19 years, Joe, 13 years, Jose, 10 years, Piro, 10 years, Sam, 10 years, Ben, 8 years.

Property forgot
To one Silver Watch
A True List of the Negroes Property
Jonathan Orr, 1797.

****

[This document most likely belongs to a Civil Action Case.]

State of North Carolina
Mecklenburg County

Know all Men by these Presents, That we David T. Caldwell and James W. Osborne all of the County of Mecklenburg are held and firmly bound unto T N Alexander Shff of our said County, in the sum of eleven Hundred Dollars current money of this State: To which payment well and truly to be made and done, we bind ourselves, our heirs, executors and administrators, jointly and severally, firmly by these presents. Sealed with our seals, and dated this 27th day of Jan Anno Domini 1842.

The Condition of the above Obligation is this, Whereas the said T N Alexander Shff hath levied an execution at the instance of Irwin and Elms on certain property of D T Caldwell consisting of negro girl named Manda and a boy named Randal & two children Martha & Caroline, and which said property, at the request of the said D T Caldwell is left in his own care and possession until the same shall be sold: Now if the said D T Caldwell and James W. Osborne shall well and truly deliver the said property herein before enumerated, to the said T N Alexander at the Court House in Charlotte on or before the 4th Monday of Feby next without damage or further hindrance, then this obligation to be void otherwise to remain in full force and virtue.

Sealed and Delivered	D.T. Caldwell	(Seal)
In Presence Of	Jas W Osborne	(Seal)
N T Alexander		

****

A List of Jurymen Chosen in Capt. Samuel Blacks Company agreeable to order of Court - November 10th 1825

Alexander Irwin, Charles Dennis, Joseph **[Blank]** Esq., James Irwin Snr., John Greer, James M. Greer, James Morris, John Williamson, William Rice, Martin Harkey, Adam Fisher, James Irwin Jur., John Stilwell, John Bain, Reuben Hood Sr., Alexander Nesbett, Robert Maxwell, Matthias McCall, Isaac C. Pelt, John McCall, Thomas McCall, James J. Maxwell, Benjamin Fincher, Duncan McCowan, Daniel McLoud, Samuel Blair, Hamilton Black, Absalom Black, John Robison, James Robison, Robert Hood, William Black Jun., Silas Kerr**[?],** Samuel Black Capt., **[Name marked out],** Phillip Cender**[?],** George A. Hart, James Brown, Robert Wilson Jur., Samuel Yandle, Zebulon Morris, Philemon Morris, Peter Kistler, John Dulin, Jesse Rodgers, James Orr Jur., William Wilson, Jeremiah Maxwell, John Orr, John C. Barr, John Irwin, Hugh Wilson, Thomas Wilson, Hugh W. Rodgers, William Black Sr., James C. Orr, George Wilson, Robert Glass, Daniel N. Hall, Samuel Hart.

Taken by Me
Philemon Morris JP

****

Receipt for Taxes from E.C. Wallace

United States of America

No. 393, Receipt for Direct Taxes for Sarah A.S. McCombs, $1.96

This is to Certify, That E.C. Wallace, Gdn. has this day paid to the undersigned the sum of One Dollar and Ninety six Cents, that being the amount in full for taxes, penalty, interest, and costs, charged under the Act of Congress, entitled "An Act for the collection of direct taxes, in insurrectionary districts within the United States, and for other purposes" approved June 7, 1862, upon the following tract or lot of Land, situate in the Co of Mecklenburg, and State of N.C., and described as follows: 54 Acres Val 245

Witness our hands, at Charlotte, this 27th day of Feby, A.D. 1866.

Hiram Potter Jr., Commissioner of Direct Taxes for --

United States of America

No. 392, Receipt for Direct Taxes for Adam M. McCombs, $2.76

This is to Certify that E.C. Wallace Gdn. has this day paid to the undersigned the sum of Two Dollars and Seventy Six Cents, that being the amount in full for taxes, penalty, interest, and costs, charged under the Act of Congress, entitled "An act for the collection of direct taxes in insurrectionary districts within the United States, and for other purposes, " approved June 7, 1862, upon the following tract or lot of Land, situate in the Co of Mecklenburg, and State of N.C., and described as follows: 46 Acres Val. 345

Witness our hands, at Charlotte, this 27th day of Feby, A.D. 1866

Hiram Potter Jr., Commissioner of Direct Taxes for ---

****

Mecklenburg County }

Personally appeared before me Jennings B. Kerr Clerk of the Superior Court for said County Robert D. Whitley and made oath in due form of law that he has been ib possession of a negro boy slave named Elic - aged about 55 or 60 years dark complexion worth about three hundred dollars within two years from the date hereof, and that he has been deprived of the possession of said Slave by John F. Pettus of said County. Sworn to & subscribed before me this 16th day of August 1862.
RD Whitley
JB Kerr Clerk SC

State of North Carolina
To the Sheriff of Mecklenburg County Greeting
Whereas Robert D. Whitley has made oath that Elic a Slave aged about 55 or 60 years of dark complexion has been in his lawful possession within two years from the date hereof, and that he has been deprived of the possession of the said Slave by John F. Pettus the defendant without his consent or permission and whereas the said Robert D. Whitley hath further made oath that the said slave is of the value of three hundred dollars and hath also given bond with approved security in the sum of six hundred dollars payable to the said John F. Pettus conditional to perform the final judgement which may be rendered in this suit of [?] & hath also given bond with security for the prosecution of the Suit.

You are therefore commanded forthwith to take the said slave into your custody if to be found in your County and deliver him to the said Plaintiff, unless the said defendant shall execute & deliver to you a bond with approved security in the Sum of Six hundred dollars payable to the said plaintiff and conditional to perform the final Judgment which shall be rendered in this suit and if the aforesaid defendant shall execute & deliver to you a bond as aforesaid you are commanded to return said bond with this suit.

You are further commanded to summon the said John F. Pettus the said defendant if to be found in your County to Appear before the Honourable Judge of our Superior Court of law to be held for the County of Mecklenburg at the Court House in Charlotte on the eleventh Monday after the fourth Monday of September next then and there to answer the said Robert D. Whitley of a plea of [?] and unjustly detain the said Slave

Mecklenburg County

Real Estate Valuation of Gray P. Hipp & Pink Hipp

State of North Carolina }
Mecklenburg County }

We the undersigned having been appointed by the County Court - to value and report the real Estate of Gray P Hipp and Pink Hipp - do value and assess the Same at ten Dollars per acre - being one hundred and Eighty acres - aggregate $1800.00.

In testimony we have set our hand & seals January 2 - 1864 - Colativol[?]
taxes $18 - 00
Wm S. Norment
Stephen Wilson
M.M. Moore

****

Confederate Tax Form
Tax in Kind
Form No. 1 Estimate No.

Estimate and Assessment of Agricultural Products which are taxed in kind, agreed upon by the Assessor and Tax Payer, and the Value of the portion thereof to which the Government is entitled in accordance with the provisions of "An Act to lay taxes for the common defence, and carry on the Government of the Confederate States," and an "Act to amend said Act, approved 17th February 1864;" said Estimate and Assessment to be returned to the District Quartermaster on or before the 1st day of September of each year.

Agricultural Products - Quantity of Gross Crops - Quality - Tithe - Value of Tithe

Wheat..

Oats..

Sheaf Oats..

Rye..

Mecklenburg County

Cured Hay..

Wool...

....Total Value, $

I________________**of the**_______________ **and**__________**do swear that** the above is a true statement and Estimate of all the Agricultural Products named produced by me during the year 186 _____which are taxable by the provisions of the above stated Acts, including what may have been used or consumed by me in the best of my knowledge and belief

____Tax Payer

Sworn to and Subscribed before me, the______day of 186___and I further certify that the above Estimate has been agreed upon by said ________and Myself as a correct and true statement of the amount of his crops, and that the value of the portion to which the Government is entitled is correctly stated.

____Assessor

_______________Tax District State of____________________

Received at Depot No._____Congressional District, State of_________

of ____________Bushels __________________ Pounds of Wheat,

______________Bushels_________Pounds of Oats,________Bushels

____________Pounds of Rye,_______Pounds of Cured Hay,______Pounds

___________Ounces of Wool ___________________of the above estimate

__________________________Agency

_________________________ day of ________186_

Special Exemptions

1. Each head of a family, not worth more than five hundred dollars

2. Each head of a family, with minor children, not worth more than five hundred dollars for himself, and one hundred dollars for each minor living with him, and five hundred dollars in addition therein for each minor son he has living, or may have lost, or had disabled in the military or naval service.
3. Each officer, soldier, or seaman, in the army or navy, or who has been discharged therefrom, for wounds, and is not worth more than one thousand dollars.
4. Each widow of any officer, soldier, or seaman, who has died in the military or naval service, the widow not worth more than one thousand dollars. Provided, the farmer or planter shall not pay a tax of kind upon corn, when he does not produce more than two hundred bushels or upon Irish potatoes when he does not produce more than fifty bushels, or upon peas and beans, when not more than twenty bushels are produced; and the forage derived from the corn plant shall also be exempt in all cases where the corn is not taxed in kind, neither shall any farmer or planter, who does not produce more than fifteen pounds ginned cotton for each member of his family, or ten pounds of wool, be subject to the tax in kind.
5. Such portion of said crops as may be necessary to raise and fatten the hogs of such farmer, planter, or grazier, for pork.

****

Copy of Vandue List
[undated]

A shovel	John Springs	.32
Abel John	Abel John	1.50
4 holds	Ditto	1.60
A grindstone	Ditto	.75
A Axe	Orrin Pierce	2.10
A foot Adze	John Stinson	.81
A small Axe	Jerry Cheek	.25
Draw Knives	Abel John	.60
A Axe	Ditto	.25
Hansaw	James Cunningham	.10
Lot of old Iron	John Stewart	2.25
Lot old chisels	Thompson Rea	.30

One Iron Wedge	Jerry Cheek	.54
A pitch fork	Moses Kerr	.38
two large Shear Ploughs	David Smith	2.00
One do do Plough	John Stewart	1.00
A Sythe	William Manson	.25
A Cutting Box	James Darnel	.51
A pair Double trus	James Cunningham	.50
two raw hides	Abel John	.35
A reving Frow	Jerry Cheek	1.00
one Stack Fodder	Peggey John	3.00
Lot Tobacco 24w @6c	Jessey Cheek	1.44
Lot Do. 28w @ 7½	John Stewart	2.10
2 Lots Do. 23:40 @ 8	Robert Cochron	3.61
Stack Fodder --	Abel John	.31
Fodder House ____	Abel John	3.00
20 bushels Corn @ 66 Cents	Jordan Potter Junr.	13.20
20 Do Do @ 64 Cents	Jordan Potter Junr.	12.80
20 Bushels - Corn - 63	Robert Porter	12.60
20 Bushels - Corn - 63	John Sharpe	12.60
10 bushels Do - 63	Peggy John	6.30
4¼ Do Do 63	Abel John	2.65
4¼ Do Do 63	James Cunningham	2.65
		55.08
A Truckle Waggon	David Smith	4.01
One Bee Gum	Peggy John	1.61
One Do Do	James Cunningham	2.00
A Sow & Pigs	Abel John	10.00
5 hogs	Jordon Potter	18.75
3 hogs	John Stewart	7.00
2 hogs	Abel John	14.00
2 Ditto	Ditto	9.25
2 bolls	Sylvester Wit**[Weil?]**	1.31
Man Saddle	John Sharpe	7.02
Side Saddle	Peggey John	11.00
Side Leather	Osborne Robinson	1.50
Side Leather	James Cunningham	1.50
One Cow	David Smith	15.03
One Cow	Abel John	14.41

One Cow	Osborn Robinson	8.25
One Negro boy	Abel John	401.00
One Ditto Girl	Peggey John	152.00
one Ditto Winch or Woman	Benjamin Massey	424.00
1 Mare	Eli Cheek	30.01
1 horse	Peggey John	50.00
4 Augurs	Moses Kerr	.51
A two horse tree	James Cunningham	.61
A Cros cut saw	**[Blank]**	
1 Clives & hook	Jerry Cheek	.30
A Do Do	Moses Kerr	.53
Six barrel	Adams Brown	1.00
A Walnut Tabel	Abel John	3.10
Five Irons	James Cunningham	3.10
A trunk	Margaret John	.12½
3 Chairs	Abel John	.70
A Cheek Reel	Peggey John	.50
A Cotton Wheel	Peggey John	1.51
		1254.44½
A Little Wheel	Willm. Mathis Esq	.70
A pair Cotton Cards	Do Do	.20
A pair Do	Peggey John	1.00
A pott rack	Abel John	1.51
A Do & hooks	Do Do	2.31
A Large Pott	Peggey John	1.00
A Small Pott	Adams Brown	1.00
A Large Skillet	Do Do	1.00
A Looking Glass	Peggey John	.56
a Pair of Wool Cards	Do Do	.50
a ½ bushel Measure	Wm. Matthews	.60
A Flax Hackel	Margaret Black	1.02
A beslar**[?]** pale	Wm Cunningham	.60
A Churn	Do Do	.12½
6 pewter plates	Andw. Rea	2.30
2 Do Dishes	Wm Cunningham	2.55
13 spoons	Abel John	1.10
6 Delph plates	Peggey John	.75
Cups & Saucers	Do Do	.75

A Lot of pewter	Jas. Cunnungham	.30
6 Tin Cups	Peggey John	.64
5 Pewter basons	Jerry Cheek	1.50
Stillards	Moses Kerr	.80½
1 Flat Iron	David Smith	.48
Knives & forks	Abel John	.61
A Candle stick	Do Do	.13
Pepper box & cup	Peggey John	.15
A Chest & Drawers	Do Do	21.10
Bed & Furniture	Do Do	21.10
Do Do	Jas Cunningham	12.60
A bed	Margaret Black	8.20
A Do & Furniture	Abel John	34.35
		1374.57
A bed Stead & Curtains	Wm. Cunningham	6.51
A hem & Chains	Abel John1	.78
A Mare & colt	Jessey Cheek	30.10
A black mare	Cilus Cheek	37.00
A bay mare	John Stewart	30.00
A bay horse	Abel John	51.50
A Gun	Wm. Cunningham	2.00
A Side Sand. Leather	Adams Brown	.70
Warping bars	Peggey John	.23
A Compass	Sylvester Weit	1.82
A Reed[?]	David Smith	.85
Do Do	John Thomas	.31
Rent of Land	Abel John	40.00
Shoe Tools	Robert Porter	2.10
A bag	Peggey Potter	1.10
A brass Kettle	Moses Kerr	.14½
A Pott rack	Robert Porter	.17½
1 jugg	Peggey John	.81
2 Do	Do Do	.05
Seed Cotton 74c @ 4 Cents	Do Do	2.96
1 hogshead	John Kinnear	.13
1 pair Kiddles	Peggy John	.31
1 pr Do	Peggy Do	.35
3 case bottles	Moses Kerr	.38¾

2 Do Do	Abel John	25½
A Case razors	Do Do	.67
A razor hone	James Cunningham	.50
A Sythe	Abel John	.05
Man Saddle	John Simmison	3.10
Cros Cut Saw	Moses Kerr	.6¼
		$1554.37

****

Estate Sale, 1821
[Name of decedent not given.]

A list of articles Sold March 9th, 1821

Persons Names	
Allison Clark to one Shot Gun	12.00
Thomson Plent**[?]** to two powder	1.26
John Prise to one Clock	16**[?]**
[Name faded] to one pare of Whet Reddels	.50
Ditto to two Whet Reddels	**[Blank]**
Richard Kerr to one Pistol & Box of Razors	.15
John Kerr to one irin Wedg	.46
Widdow to one **[?]** & Harnes	25.10
Wm A. McGee to one hog	7.00
Widdow to one Sow	2.00
Widdow to one Sow & **[?]**	1.97
Widdow to two shots two **[?]**	3.51
Widdow to 3 choise of hogs	3.52
Alexander McClure to 4 Choise of hogs	2.82
Widdow to two first of eighteen Jugs	.50
Alexander McClure to 4 Choise Pigs	2.40
Caleb Caps to 2 Choise of Pigs	2.52
Ms Cilly to 3 Choise of pigs	2.41
Samuel Martin to 4 Choise of hogs	2.30
Widdow to one scilit	1.00
Widdow to one fire shovel	.50
Dito to one Pot & **[?]**	.50

Dito to one shovel plow	.50
Dito to one Dubeltres	.65
Mrs Cilly to one shovel Shere	.25
Widow to one Barsher	1.00
Mrs Celly to one Coller Plow	.50
James Thomson to one log chean	2.10
James Thomson to one Syth and Credal	**[Blank]**
John Prise to one Sproutin how	.81
Widdow to one lot of hows	1.00
Widdow to one Bees Cap	1.00
Widdow to two Beas Caps	.25
Richard Kerr to one steel trap	2.00
Jas. Bradley to one steel trap	2.20
[Blank] to one frow	**[Blank]**
James Nolen to two augurs	.30
Widdow to one 3 quart eraugur	.12½
James Thompson to one Box of Copper	3.00
Alexander McClure to two pare of horse Shoes	.76
Allxr McClure to two horse shoes	.6¼
Jas Thomson to two Jointers	.50
Jas Thomson to two plains	.25
Widow to one draw knife	.25
Jas Hunter to two S Chane	.50
[?] Kerr to one axe	.58
Widdow to one axe	.58
Mrs Celly to one axe	.81
Widdow to one han saw	.12½
Widdow to one hand saw	.15
Widdow to one ireon	.25
James Bradley to iron By the Pounds 6¼	
Wm McCord to Iron By the P 6¼	
Widdow to one pare of Canes and Coler	.50
Widdow to 2 Barrels	.25
Widdow to 1 Barrel	.25
Widdow to one Loom	5.00
Widdow to 2 Barrels	.17½
Widdow to Grine Stone	.12½
Widdow to one hide	1.00

Widdow to one bag	.25
Widdow to one B---	.12½
Widdow to one Bedstead	1.00
Widdow to Saddle & Bridles	.65
Widdow to 1 Bay Mare	20.00
Widdow to 1 Sorrel Mare	68.00
Widdow to one Red Cow	7.81
Wm Simons to one Cow and Calf	8.00
Wm Lemons to one Bell Cow	12.25
Widdow to one Bell	.12½
Widdow to one Red and White Cow	8.45
Thomson Plunk to one Bull	7.20
Jas Thomson to one hefer Calf	2.25
Jas Lemon to one Gun	.60
Widdow to two Sheep	2.25
Caleb Caps to two Sheep	3.00
Wm Simons to two Sheep	2.50
Richard Kerr to two Sheep	2.50
Wm Simons to two Sheep	1.50
Widow to one Cut in Box Knife	.25
Widdow to one Barel	.32
Jas Thomson to one Barel & Barley	1.35
Jas Thomson to ond lot of Rusnips	7.50

By the Seady Cotin 3½

Thomas McGin hive [?]	
Widdow Sevin Gees	2.00
William A [?] gin	8.3½
Sarah Thompson 4 Sheep Taters	4.32
William McCord to one bushel of Rounds	.52½

****

Tax received to pay County debt to Railroad Co., 1862

Rec'd of E.C. Grier former Sheriff of Mecklenburg, Five Hundred Dollars in part of the amount due for Taxes levied for the payment of the Countys indebtedness to the Wil., Char., & Rutherford R.R. Co.

$550 Nov. 15, /62 Jn Hutchison
Co. Agent

****

Collectors for the 1845 Tax List

1. Capt James M. Kerr's Company Tax List 1845
2. Capt John C. Kirkpatricks Company Tax List 1845
3. Steel Creek Company Tax List 1845
4. Capt George Campbells Company Tax List 1845
5. Jno. M. Earnhardt Company Tax List 1845
6. Duese
7. Youngs
8. Grays
9. Dennis
10. S.B. Halls
11. Lemlys

Samuel J. Lowrie
B Oates CCC

****

Tax Receipt

Received of John Simmarman
Ten Dollars
City Tax for 1868
E.H. Bissell for Wm. M. Martin, Tax Collector

****

Tax Receipt

Recd of Gilbert Cowells[?] ninrty Cents in full of taxes for the Year 1834
Wm. Wilson DC

****

List of Justices of the Peace Appointed to take Tax Returns, 1830

Mecklenburg County May Sessions 1830

To the Sheriff of Mecklenburg County Greeting You are hereby required to make Known to the under named Justices of the peace that they were appointed by Court to take the returns of Taxables in their respective Companies for the Year 1830.

To Wit
1. Brawly Oats Esqr. in the Town Company
2. Guy Maxwell Esqr. in Capt. James Blacks Company.
3. Abel Nelson Esqr. in Capt. Alexander H. Ingrams Do
4. Philemon Morris Esqr. in Capt. Zebulon Morris Do
5. Thomas O. Black Esqr. in Silas Orr's Do
6. Uriah Helms Esqr. in Capt. Belks Do
7. James Gribble Esqr. in Capt. John Blacks Do
8. Benjamin Morrow Esqr. in Capt. Mansons Do
9. Alexander Jetton Esqr. in Capt. John Caldwells Do
10. William Osborn Esqr. in Capt. John Rosses Do
11. Andrew Greer Esqr. in Capt. James Sloan Do

[The rest of this page is torn away.]

****

List of Justices of the Peace Appointed to Take Tax Returns, 1826

State of North Carolina
To the Sheriff of Mecklenburg County Greeting
You are hereby required to make known to the undernamed Justices of the Peace that they are appointed to take the returns of Taxables for the Year 1826 in the Several Captains Companies herein named to wit.

+ Adam Cooper Esqr. in Captain John Sloans Company
+ William Campbell Esqr. in Captain J. Sloans Do.
+ Alexander Greer Esqr. in Captain Saml. Meachams Do.
+ William H. McLeary Esqr. in Captain John McLearys Do.
+ William White Esqr. in Captain William Stinsons Do.
+ Benjamin Morrow Esqr. in Captain Stephen Mansons Do.
+ William Barnett Esqr. in Captain James Steels Do.
+ James G. Torrence Esqr. in Captain Harrys old Do.
+ Jacob Alexander Esqr. in Captain Bains old Do.
William Houston Esqr. in Captain Robert Lewis's Do.
William Pyron Esqr. in Captain Stewarts Do.
William Osborn Esqr. in Captain William Howie's Do.
James Belk Esqr. in Captain Belks Do.
James Cunningham Esqr. in Captain John Blacks Do.
Philemon Morris Esqr. in Captain Samuel Blacks Do.
Hugh J. McCain Esqr. in Captain Walkers Do.
Philander Alexander Esqr. in Captain Kerr's Do.

Herein they are not to fail and make due return thereof in Alphabetical Order as by Law required.

Witness Isaac Alexander Clerk of said Court at Charlotte the 4th Monday of May 1826
Isaac Alexander CMC

****

Amount of Tax Returns for the Year 1792

Oct 20th 1792 this certifies the within £811:0 - is the whole State Tax due for 1792.

£811 -0 - 2 Total
5 -8 - 1 deduct for delinquents } J.M. Alexander
£805: 12 - 1 Total due Test } Wm. Wilson
from Mr. Harris to the Treasurer } [?] Alexander
including all Commissions &c }

A List of Taxes Received from the Different Collectors, 1792

Danl. Garritt -	Plilers Company	£35 - 18 -
	Howies	34-15-7
	Porters	42-6-5
	Flanigans	34-9-8
	Osbornes	24-1-7
	Parks	66-10-0
	Alexanders	48-8-7
	Rodgers	15-17-
	Tygarts	44-18-5
	Shins	39-5-8
	Reesse	43-9-
	Davidsons	48-1-4
	Knoxes	40-17-5
	Belks	8-19-10
	Mc Neeltys	56-4-11
	Charlotte Commsr.	96-10-3
	Gardners	51-13-3
	Wylies	39-5-10
	Perkins	39-6-7
		£811-0-2

****

Appointment of Tax Collector in Capt. Young's Company, 1843

State of North Carolina }
Mecklenburg County }

This day personally appeared John Kirk before us two of the acting Justices of the Peace in & for said County and having been Employed by Thos. N. Alexander High Sheriff of the County, and parish Taxes for Capt. Young's Company took an oath faithfully and honestly to account for all moneys that may be received by him in the Capacity of a Collector.

In Testimony whereof we have hereunto set our hands and seals this 28th June 1843.

C.J. Tap**[Tos?]** JP (Seal)
A. Alexander JP (Seal)

****

Town Property Assessors for the Year 1826

Mecklenburg County
To the Sheriff of Mecklenburg County Greeting:
You are hereby required to make known to Robert J. Dinkins, Green Kendrick and David Parks that they are appointed assessors of Town property for the Tax of the Year 1826 and that they assess the Same as soon as Convenient and make return thereof into the Clerks Office.
Witness
Isaac Alexander CCC

****

Amount of Taxes for Year 1792

Mecklenburg County }
October Term 1794 }

This may Certify that the Publick Tax for the Year 1792 of said County is Eight Hundred and five Pounds twelve shillings and one penny.
Jas Martin CM

****

Taxable Property of Capt. B.F. Browns Company -- 1844

List of the Taxable property of Capt. B.F. Browns Company for the year 1844.

	Acres	Value	Wt Poles	B Ps
Adams, John W.	100	350	1	
Armstrong, Nancy	47	225		
Burihill, D.W.			1	
Bigham, William	156	936		

Bigham, Lawson H.			1	
Bigham, Samuel	104	260		
Bigham, Robert M.			1	
Boyd, Joseph B.	100	200	1	
Beaty, James M.			1	
Beaty, John	133	665		3
Beaty, Ann	70	380		1
Beaty, William	83	250		3
Beaty, John A.			1	
Beaty, Francis M.	234	1085		2
Burihill, Samuel	120	360	1	2
Brown, Allen F.	60	180	1	
Brown, Benjamine F.	160	480	1	
Byram, John P.			1	
Beaty, Alexander			1	
Clark, Andrew	50	100		
Cooper, William	150	600		2
Cooper, Alexander Esqr.	511	1647		2
Cathy, Archibald	50	150	1	
Cathy, George Sen.	140	280		
Cathy, George C.	128	258	1	
Cathy, George			1	
Cathy, Alexander	90	360		
Cathy, William	51	102	1	
Carson, Robert			1	
Clark, William	221	679		
Cook, Margaret	351	892		3
Clanton, Elinor	50	250		1
Cathcart, James L.	210	785		
Cathcart, John	102	382		
Cathcart, Robert	139	490	1	
Emerson, Thomas	163	489	1	
Fulwood, Samuel M.	112	336	1	1
Freeman, William			1	
Herron, John W.	400	500		1
Herron, William			1	
Herron, Allen	140	420		
Hayes, D.C.	114	285	1	
Hoover, Phillip	233	1665		3

Griffith, **[Faded]**	**[?]**	1137		
Greer, Andrew Esqr.	680	3600		19
Jimason, William	444	1221		6
Jimason, Andrew	**8[?]**	190		
Jimason, William J.			1	
Johnston, Alexander	104	203	1	
Johnston, John			1	
Kerr, William F.			1	
Kerr, Robert M.	116	300	1	
McKnight, John N.			1	
McKnight, James M.			1	
McKnight, Executor of Robert	150	677		
McCay, Edmund A.	232	1072	1	
McAlister, James			1	
Montgomery, Wilson			1	
McCorkle**[?],** D.P.			1	
Marshell, James	279	737		1
Marshell, William	150	493	1	
Marshell, James H.	129	366	1	
McKnight, Robert H.	129	508	1	
McDowell, Robert J.	402	2200	1	4
McDowell, Rebecca	132	887		4
McDowell, Robert W.	104	624	1	3
McDonald, G.W.	366	1177	1	2
McDonald, Exect. of David	140	295		1
Nicholson, Joseph C.	50	108	1	
Ormand, Andrew	112	392	1	1
Owen, Sarah	64	392		
Owen, William			1	
Porter, Alexander	191	764		
Porter, Margaret & Sarah	130	260		
Porter, A.M.C.			1	
Porter, John M.			1	
Porter, James	344	1005		7
Porter, T.F.			1	
Porter, James L.	200	800	1	1
Porter, John	129	654		
Porter, William N.	200	800	1	

Parks, Elisabeth	340	1200		3
Parks, William N.	342	1024		10
Parks,one stud horse	[?] six Dollars			1
Roddan, Andrew	56	186	1	
Reid, R.W.			1	1
Ray, Midelton			1	
Ray, Adm. of James	520	2340		
Roddan, John			1	
Roddan, Thomas			1	
Reid, William K. Guardian for Male heirs of David [?]				
	460	2070		
Reid, Samuel	200	700		
Reid, John			1	
Stewart, James Adm. of Robert Collans				
	210	525		
Smith, J[?T] H	150	450	1	
Sandifer, T.T.	170	655	1	2
Suggs, William			1	
Sloan, George S.	240	1516	1	2
Sloan, James M.	183	732	1	3
Sloan, Robert	216	714	1	3
Smith, Benjamine R.	520	2125	1	5
Spratt, Ann	30	115		
Sadler, A.F.	390	1170	1	9
Tevepaug, John	2[?]0	500		
Tevepaug, Samuel	50	125	1	
Tevepaug, Philip			1	
Warren, Richard	**[Faded]**	318		1
Williamson, G.W.	**[Faded]**	682	1	5
Waddle, Archibald	**[Faded]**	364		1

I Certify that this taxes contain a true List of the taxable Property of Capt. B.F. Browns Company for the year 1844.
John Sloan JP
Browns Compy., 1844, Recorded, Page 130

****

Mecklenburg County

Tax Returns for 1780 & 1781

The Amount of Taxes Received from the **[Faded]** Collectors for the Years 1780 and 1781
[Faded] Colecter for Capt Wylie Compt 25194

[Faded] McCorkel	Fosters	29005
[Faded] Wallace	Gardners	20513-3
David Reese	Rees	33984
[Faded] Alexander	Alexander	24050-14-5
[Faded] Caruth	McAnullys	21554-12-4
[Faded] [Faded]	Davies	14242-4-4
Conrad Houe	Houes	10039-10-1
Daniel Jarrett	Plilars	10030-7-3
Isaak Williams	McKnights	22479-0
John Belk	Rodgers	5822-8
Archibald Houston	Pickens	22099-5-5
Francis Moor	Brounfields	28000-0-**[?]**
John McKnit Alexander	Knox	29860-4-10
Saml. Blythe	Potts	27075
James Jack	Charlotte	19560-11
Neal Morrison	Flanigans	31264-12-0
		£389774-12-0
Deduct for County poor tax		2062
Total		387712-12-0

This certifies the above is the true estimate of State Tax due for 1780 & 1781, Octr. 18th 1781
By, J.M.L. Alexander, Wm. Wilson & M **[?]** Alexander

£387712-12-0
6365-9-0 for delinquents
£381347-3-0 Totals of State

Tax for 1780 & 1781 including Commissions of 5 per cent to Thomas Harris - &c - JMLA

****

Mecklenburg County

Certification of Taxes Returned, 1763

1763 Dls. the publick of North Carolina - to Mr. Alexander Lewis, Sheriff of Mecklinburg County.

To 90 Delinquents allowed me on Settelments with the Court for ye year of 63 at 7/2d Each 32:5:0

My Commission on Collacting } 14: 16-6 of 246: 3.6

Cash paid the Treasurer 246 -3-6
£293-5-0

By 777 Taxables for ye year of 1763 at } 278:8 : 6
7/2 Each } 14: 16 :6
with my Commission on Collacting } £293:5:0
[Next section of page torn and missing]

Ballance Alexander Lewis on a full Settlment 210:0:0

This may certifie that Alexander Lewis late Sherif of McLenburg has paid for the whole number of Taxables on the List without any Allowance for Insolvents for the year 1763 which has been settled & paid by him to the Public.
Nov. 1763 Jno. Ashe **[?]**

****

Certification of the Amount of Taxes, 1763

Mecklenburg County }
This day Personally before me Came Alexander Lewis Esqr. late High Sherif of the County aforesaid and being duly Examined on the Holy Evangelists of Almighty God doth depose and say that the above Accompt of debt and Credit is a Just & True State of His the said Lewis Accompts as High Sheriff for the County aforesaid for the year 1763.

Sworn to and Subscribed } Alexr. Lewis

this 27th October A.D. 1768 }
Robt. Harris

****

Certification of the Amount of Taxes, 1780 & 1781

Mecklenburg County: October 1784

This Certifies that the amount of the State Tax for the years 1780 & 1781 amounts to three Hundred & Eighty one thousand three hundred and forty seven pounds three shillings
£381, 347 - 3 - 0
By Ja Martin CMC

****

Tax Delinquents for the Year 1802.

A List of delinquents on the Tax Lists of the County of Mecklenburg for the Year 1802

Jonathan Malawn	on. p.	--1--
John Eakins		--1--
James Pucket		--1--
Margaret Greer 150 acres of Land not to be found		-- -- 6
Christopher Love	one p	--1--
Daniel McGinnis		--1--
James Price		--1--
Josiah Price		--1--
Thos Ramey		--1--
Francis Youngblood	3 p	--3--
William Alexander		--1--
Stephen Alexander		--1--
Dan Alexander		--1--
Saml Martin		--1--
Thos Neely		--1--

James Simons	--1--
James Cayrel	--1--
Thos Rogers	--1--
Robt Thompson	--1--
William Wilson	--1--
James R. Alexander	--1--
James Allon	--1--
Joseph Cannen Jun.	--1--
John Jinkens	--1--
John Hightower **[Marked through]**	
150 Acres of Land Charged to Alexr Ross &	
Colo William Hill both	-- --6
Noah Woodruff	--1--
Nath Hurington	--1--
James Kennady a twofold Tax	--2--
	£1 - 10 - 0
Adley Flanigan	--1--
Andrew Wilson	--2--
	£1 - 13 - 0

****

Notification to Tax Collectors for 1782

Mecklenburg County July Session 1782

To the sherif, You are hereby Required to Notify the following named persons Appointed Collectors for the present Year.

Viz

Geo Elliot of Capt	Knoxs Compy
Leonard Garvis	Hills
Daniel Garrett	Plilers
Adam Alexander	McCurdys
James Wetherspoon	Flinnikins
Adam Meek	Garners
John Allison	Reeses
Wm Patterson	Jacks

[The rest of this page is torn and missing]

of their several Duties thereunto **[Smeared]** that they call for their several Lists of Tax at the Clerks Office immediately.
Herein fail not &c
Witness Jam Martin
20th March 1783

****

Tax Returns for Capt. Amos Alexander's Company, 1843

A List of the Returns of the taxable property in Capt Amos Alexanders Company for the year 1843

Name	Acres	Val.	Wt. Poles	B Poles
Alexander, Dr Cyrus Exr of J.T.J. Orr	364	1480		
Alexander, Markes	130	455	1	
Alexander, Siles	245	857	1	3
Augustus Col.	373	1840		7
Alexander, Charles G.	150	750	1	3
Alexander, George M.	192	495	1	4
Alexander, Darkes C.	58	174		
Alexander, John S.	121	363		
Alexander, William A.	126	378	1	
Alexander, Susanah widow	163	815	2	
Alexander, Amos, Capt.	186	372	1	
Alexander, Do. as Admr. of William S., Dec'd	96	480		
Alexander, Hezekiah C.			1	
Alexander Mrs. Susan				
Alexander, Clem C.			1	
Alexander, Thomas W. Admrs.	40	200		
Alexander, James M.			1	
Alexander, Tina	43	172	1	
Allen, Robert M.			1	
Brown, Cyrus			1	
Brown, William			1	
Brown, Charles	30	120	1	

Brown, John	115	150		
Biggins, William C.			1	
Bays, Elam B.	175	1050	1	
Bays, Samuel A.	430	1572	1	
Baker, George	293	1000		
Black, Absalom	262	327		1
Black, William			1	
Bays, Mrs. Ann	192	886		3
Bales, Eli	129	645	1	
Cammel, John A.			1	1
Cowan, David			1	
Chambers, David	278	1222		3
Combs, John A.			1	
Davis, Samuel A.	257	1285	1	6
Davis, Do. Admr of William Blackwood Dec'd	47	117		
Dinkins, Lewis	1170	4680		13
Elliot, Samuel H. Esqr.	694	2912	1	9
Elliot, Do. Executor of B. Weathers	40	120		
Ellems, John	129	796	1	2
Fergeson, Francis			1	
Fergeson, Abner			1	
Flaniken, John O.			1	2
Flaniken, Mary	181	1086		
Flaniken, Lee B.			1	
Guger[?], Alexander			1	
Griffeth, Aaron H.	136	408	1	1
Greer, Isaac	194	582	1	5
Hall, Eli	100	400	1	
Hutchison, John M.			1	
Hays, Joseph	105	525		
Kerr, Samuel	80	160	1	
Kerr, James	50	200		
Kerr, Samuel Junr.			1	
Kirkpatrick, Thomas	467	1864		3
Kirkpatrick, Robert G.			1	
Kirkpatrick, Margaret	600	1200		1

Kirkpatrick, John C.				1
Kirkpatrick, Hugh	275	1126	1	9
Kirkpatrick, Margaret G.	100	600		2
Kirkpatrick, Robert (Major)	347	1450		
Kirkpatrick, Samuel H.	217	651	1	1
Kenady, Harvy	200	500	1	3
Kenady, Do Guardian for E Weeks	200	800		
Lee, David M.	376	1818	1	6
Lee, Do for E.C. Sprot	353	2237		5
Lee, William	218	1360	1	4
Lee, John N. home Track	100	400	1	
Lee, Do Kirkpatrick Track	100	600		
Lee, Do Paw Creek Track	136	340		
Morrow, David			1	1
McColoch, John	410	1810		10
McCoughlen, Samuel	90	360	1	
Mulwee, John Junr.	80	160	1	
Manson, Margaret	425	1557		5
Neagle, Mathew	265	1060	1	2
Orr, Nathan	361	1289		8
Orr, Joab			1	1
Orr, Do Guardn for the heirs of W. Cook	260	780		
Orr, Jonathin			1	
Porter, Cathern	94	282		
Phifer, David N.			1	
Potts, James A.G.	84	504		
Parks, John M.	287	1840	1	4
Patterson, Joseph home track	366	2928	1	7
Patterson, Do The old Place	343	1035		
Philips, West				
Rusel, Thomas	24	48	1	
Rusel, Sarah	11	22		
Rusel, James			1	
Ross, Joseph M. Sr.	601	2299		10
Ross, William home Place	395	1882		15
Ross, Do Wifes Land	647	2571		
Ross, Do Grd for William Potter	28	112		
Ross, Do J.P. Ross Land	310	930		

Ross, Do Trustee for the [?] of				
John Patterson	700	3500		
Ross, James N.	90	720	1	
Rea, Mary	62	217		1
Reavs, William				4
Reed, William, Capt.	510	1877	1	5
Reid, John B. Withes	500	3000	1	4
Reid, John Admr. of Joseph Dec'd	1164	4564	1	11
Scarlot, George			1	
Steward, Elizabeth	81	243		
Sturgon, Letty	40	200		2
Sampel, James			1	
Stanford, Moses T.			1	
Smith, Samuel H. Sr.	320	1280		3
Tredencek, Nickles	310	790	1	2
Tredencek, Richard	300	739	1	
Taylor, William D.			1	
Walker, John Capt.	383	1480	1	10
Walker, Do Guard, pr Son James	195	585		
Walker, Elizabeth	100	400		
Weeks, Joseph	395	1750	1	6
Weeks, John	234	1020	1	5
Weeks, Nancy	160	800		
Wilson, James, Sheriff	300	1500		12
Watson, Samuel B. Sr.	285	1710	1	3
The Estate of Martha Kirkpatrick				
Dec'd	50	50		

I Certify the four going to be Corect as given in to me
Wm. Ross JP
Recorded page 44, Book 1844
Capt. Amos Alexanders Company

Chapter Ten

Gaston County

Criminal Actions

State Vs. Samuel Winter [1860]
Criminal Action
Harboring a Slave
Gaston County

State Vs Samuel Winter
Indictment, "Harboring Slave"
True Bill, Miles Hoffman
F.M.
D.A. Pros & Witn
Witnesses: JH Ramsour, Wm. C. Goforth, J Hardin, AJ Falls, Roxanna Falls, Margaret Adams X & M.W. Adams X . Those marked X thus Sworn & sent.
A. Ford CCC
by JG Lewis Dept.

State of North Carolina } Court of Pleas & Quarter Sessions
Gaston County } August Term 1860

The Jurors for the State upon their oath do present that Samuel Winter of the county and state aforesaid, in the County of Gaston with force and arms one negro slave, named Rufus, the property of David A. Jenkins, being at the time a runaway, on the 1st day of January 1860 and on divers other times before and after said day, did harbor and maintain contrary to the statute in such cases made and provided and against the peace and dignity of the state.

And the Jurors aforesaid, upon their oath aforesaid do present that, Samuel Winter aforesaid in the county aforesaid, at the time aforesaid with force and arms did entice, persuade and tempt a negro slave called Rufus the property of D.A. Jenkins, then and there in his possession, to absent himself from his owners service contrary to the statute in such cases made and provided and against the peace and dignity of the State.
Waters, Sol.

****

State Vs. Robert W. Winter [1860]
Criminal Action
Harboring a Slave
Gaston County

State Vs. Robert W. Winter
Indictment, Harboring a Slave
D.A. Jenkins, Pros & **[Faded]**
Witnesses: J. Hardin, W.C. Goforth & James Quinn
Amzi **[?]** CCC
True Bill, Miles Hoffman

State of North Carolina }
Gaston County }

To any lawful officer of said County Greeting:
Whereas information hath come to me that Robert W. Winters a citizen of this county hath been guilty of trading with a slave, Rufus the property of DA Jenkins, These are therefore to command you to arrest the said Robert W Winters and bring him before me or some other acting Justice of the Peace to answer said charge.
Herein fail not, Given under my hand & seal this 8 June 1860.
Saml. Jarratt**[?]** (Seal)
J Hardin, Wit.

June 8 1860

The within Case was returned before us this day and on examination of J. Hardin who says that Mr Winter acknowledged to buying the leather from DA Jenkins runaway negro & Dft admits the charge thereupon we require Deft to enter into Bond of five hundred dollars for his appearance at our next County Court Wm Adams entered recognizance with prisoner in the required Bonds.
J Froneburg JP
Saml Jaritt JP
State Vs Robt Winter, Executed
Jas Lusk[?] by G Gamble
May 8, 1860, Judgment for executing this Warrant

Warrant	40
Summoning Witness	20
	60

J Froneburger JP

State of North Carolina }Court of Pleas & Quarter Sessions
Gaston County }August Term 1860

The Jurors for the State upon their oath do present that Robert W. Winter, late of said county with force and arms, in the county of Gaston one negro slave named Rufus, the property of D.A. Jenkins at the time being a runaway, on the 1st day of January 1860 and divers other days and times in said county, did harbor and maintain, contrary to the statute in such case made and provided and against the peace and dignity of the State.

And the Jurors aforesaid upon their oath aforesaid, do present that Robert W. Winter in the county of Gaston on the 1st of January 1860 and other times, with force and arms, one negro slave named Rufus the property of DA Jenkins at that time in his possession, did entice persuade and tempt to leave and absent himself from his masters service contrary to the statute in such case made and provided and against the peace and dignity of the State.
Waters, Sol.

State of North Carolina.
To the Sheriff of Gaston County Greeting:

Gaston County

You are hereby commanded to take the body of Robert W. Winters if to be found in your County, and him safely keep, so that you have him before the Justices of our County Court of Pleas and Quarter Sessions, at the next Court, to be held for the County of Gaston at the Court House in Dallas, on the third Monday in february next, then and there to answer a charge of the State, Harboring a Slave.

Herein fail not; and have you then and there this Writ.

Witness, Amzi Ford, Clerk of our said Court, at Office, the 3rd Monday in August and in the 85th year of our Independence, A.D. 1860. Issued the 1st day of February, 1861.
Amzi Ford CCC
per M.L. Ford DC

To hand the 2 of feb 1861
J Lusk Shff
State Vs. Robt. Winter, Harboring a Slave
To Feby Sep 1861
Due Search made and to be found in my county
J Lusk Shff

****

State Vs. S. Kenly [1862]
Criminal Action
Gaston County

State of North Carolina } Court of Pleas & Quarter Sessions
Gaston County } Aug Term, 1862
Ms Ann Kennedy Charges the State for attending as a witness in this suit

1 days at 60 cts per day	.60
8 Miles traveling	.06
Ferriage	.10
	.76

Sworn to before me, at Office, this 18 day Aug 1862
MD Glenn CCC

Chapter Eleven

Union County

CIVIL ACTIONS

William Bibb VS. Jonathan B. Hart [1851]
Civil Action
Union County

William Bibb Vs. J.B. Hart
State of North Carolina, County Court Office

We, the subscribers, do jointly and severally bind ourselves, our heirs, executors and administrators, in the sum of one hundred Dollars to J.B. Hart, heirs, executors, administrators and assigns. The obligation to be void on condition that Wm Bibbs do prosecute a certain suit brought in the Court aforesaid, by Wm. Bibb against JB Hart and in case of failure, shall pay the said JB Hart such costs and damages as may be awarded against the said W. Bibb by the court having cognizance thereof.

Witness our hands and seals, the 14 day of October 1850.
William Bibb (Seal)

State of North Carolina
To the Sheriff of Union County, Greeting:

You are hereby commanded to take the body of J.B. Hart if to be found in your county, and him safely keep, so that you have him before the Justices of our County Court of Pleas and Quarter Sessions, at the next Court to be held for the county of Union at the Court House in Monroe on the 1st Monday in January next, then and there to answer Wm. Bibb of a Plea of Trespass on the case to his damage three hundred Dollars. Herein fail not; and have you then and there this writ.

Witness, JM Stewart Clerk of our said Court, at Office, the 1st Monday in October and in the seventy 5th year of our Independence, A.D. 1850
JM Stewart Clk

State of North Carolina }
Union County }

Know all men by these presents, That we, Jonathan B Hart and William W. Hart all of the county aforesaid, are held and firmly bound unto Darling Rushing, Sheriff of Union County, in the just and full sum of Six hundred Dollars current money of the State aforesaid, to be paid unto the said Darling Rushing, Sheriff as aforesaid, as such Sheriff, his heirs, executors, administrators or assigns, jointly and severally, firmly by these presents. Sealed with our seals, and dated this 16 day of Oct A.D. 1850.

The Condition of the above Obligation is such, That if the above bounden Jonathan B Hart who has been arrested by the said Darling Rushing Sheriff as aforesaid, upon a writ returnable to the next County Court for Union county, at the suit of William Bibb do well and truly make his personal appearance at our next county Court to be holden for the county of Union on the 1st Monday of January next, then and there to answer unto the said Wm Bibb of a plea of Trespass on the Case to his Damage three hundred Dollars and then and there stand to and abide by the judgment of the said Court, and not depart the said Court without leave; and the said **[Blank]** the security of the said Jonathan B. Hart well and truly discharge himself as special of the said JB Hart in the said Court; then the above obligation to be void, otherwise to remain in full force and effect.

Signed, Sealed and Delivered } J.B. Hart (Seal)
in the Presence of }W.W. Hart (Seal)
[?] Draffin

To Darling Rushing, Sheriff of the County of Union do hereby assign over the above obligation and condition to William Bibb the plaintiff therein named, his executors and administrators to sue for and recover, agreeably to an Act of Assembly in such case made and provided. Given under my hand and seal, this 28th day of November 1850

D. Rushing Shff (Seal)

William Bibb Vs JB Hart, Clerk Case
To January Term 1851
Executed, D. Rushing, Shff

W. Bibb Vs J.B. Hart
Subpa for Plff
W.C. Steele to April Term 1851
Executed, D. Rushing, Shff

State of North Carolina.
To the Sheriff of Union County, Greeting:

You are hereby commanded to Summon W.C. Steele personally to be and appear before the Justices of our County Court of Pleas and Quarter Sessions, at the next Court to be held for our said County, at the Court House in Monroe on the 1st Monday in April next, then and there to testify, and the truth to say, in behalf of William Bibb in a certain matter of controversy before said Court depending, and then and there to be tried, wherein William Bibb is plaintiff, and Jonathan B. Hart is defendant. And this you shall in no wise omit, under penalty prescribed by law.

Witness, J. M. Stewart, Clerk of our said Court at Office the 1st Monday in Jany and in the seventy 5th year of American Independence A.D. 1851
JM Stewart Clk.

This is to show that I am Due Wm Bibbs Two Hundred dollars, Seventy five dollars is to be paid in a note on **[?]** & Hart & the Remainder in Cash in payment of Negroe girl Riner
J.B. Hart

****

William G. Winchester Vs. J.B. Hart [1850]
Civil Action
Union County

October the 18th 1850 then A True Copy of this Note
Delivered D Rushing, Shff
B C Austin DS

State of North Carolina }
Union County }

Mr WF Windle Sir you will please take Note there on first Monday in January Next at the Court House in Monroe before the Court of Pleas and Quarter sessions I Shall Return an attachment before said Court wherein William G Winchester is plaintiff and J.B. Hart is defendant when and where you are summoned to appear as Guarnished and answer on oath in Relation to what your on indebted to the Defendant and what property and effects you have in your hand, or had at the time of Receiving this Note belonging to the Defendant and also whether you know of any Debt owing to the Defendant Remaining in the hands of any other person.
October the 18th 1850
D Rushing Shff
C Austin DS

Know all men by these presents that we Jonathan B. Hart and John McCollam are held and firmly bound unto Darling Rushing Sheriff of Union County his executors administrators and assigns in the sum of Four hundred & twenty four 20/100 Dollars to the payment of which well and truly to be made and done we bind ourselves our heirs executors and administrators jointly and severally firmly by these presents Signed with our hands and sealed with our seals this the 21st day of November AD 1850.

The condition of the above obligations is such that whereas the said Jonathan B. Hart has this day replevied the following articles of property Viz Four negro slaves named Selah or Cely, Tom, Phillis and Margaret or Martha and his funds in the hands of William F Windle

Garnished **[Blank]** which were lately seized by virtue of an attachment at the instance of William G Winchester returnable to the Court of Pleas and Quarter Sessions to be held for the County of Union before a Justice of the Peace at the Court House in Monroe on the first Monday of January next.

Now therefore if the said Jonathan B. Hart shall well and truly appear before the said Court to which said Attachment is returnable and shall abide by and perform and satisfy the order and judgment of said Court then the above obligation to be void otherwise to remain in full force and effect. JB Hart (Seal)

Test JM Stewart John McCollum (Seal)

State of North Carolina }
Union County }

William G Winchester maketh oath before me Wm. H. Simpson one of the acting Justices of the peace in & for said County that Jonathan B. Hart is justly indebted to him in the sum of Two hundred & Twelve 13/100 dollars or thereabouts to the best of knowledge & belief And this Affiant has reason to believe & does believe that the said JB Hart has absconded or removed from said County or so concealed himself that the ordinary process of Law cannot be served on him.

Sworn to & subscribed before me this 18th day of Oct. 1850.

W.G. Winchester (Seal)
Test WH Simpson, JP

State of North Carolina
Union County

Know all men by these presents that we William G Winchester & GW Helms are held & firmly bound unto Jonathan B. Hart in the sum of four hundred & Twenty five & 26/100 dollars to the true and faithfull payment of which we bind ourselves are heirs executors & administrators jointly and severally by these presents signed with our hands & sealed with our seals this the 18th October 1850.

The Condition of the above is such that whereas the above bounden William G Winchester has this day served out an attachment at his own suit returnable to the Court of Pleas & Quarter Sessions against the Estate of Jonathan B Hart for the sum Two hundred twelve 13/100 dollars now therefore if the said Wm G. winchester shall prosecute the said suit with effect as in case he fail therein shall therein well & truly pay to the said JB Hart all such cost and damages as shall be hereafter be uncovered against him the said J.B. Hart for wrongfully serving out an attachment then the above obligation to be Void otherwise to remain in full force and effect.

Witness our hands & seals this the 18th of October 1850.

Test WH Simpson, JP W.G. Winchester (Seal)
G.W. Helms (Seal)

Whereas William G. Winchester hath complained on oath to me William H Simpson one of the acting Justices pf the Peace in & for said County that Jonathan B Hart is justly indebted to him in the sum of Two hundred Twelve 13/100 dollars due by book account and that the said Jonathan B Hart hath absconded or removed from the said County or so conceals himself that the ordinary Process of Law Cannot be served on him and the said William G Winchester having given bond accordingly to law.

These are therefore to command you to attach the Estate of the said Jonathan B Hart replevable as security if to be found in your County or so much thereof as shall be of value sufficient to satisfy the said debt & cost. And such Estate so attached in your hands to secure & so **[Torn]** that it shall be liable and answerable **[Torn]** to the satisfaction of the above olsi**[?]** And that you make return of your proceedings before the Court of Please and Quarter Sessions to be held for the County of Union at the Court house in the Town of Monroe on the 1st Monday of January next in order thus further proceedings may be had in relations thereto according to Law so as to compell the Defendant to appear & answer the plaintiff in the premises.

And have you then & there this writ, Herein fail not Given under my hand & seal this the 18th October AD 1850.

Summons as Garnishee WH Simpson, JP (Seal)
Wm. F Windell

October the 18th 1850 Then Levied this Attachment for Four Negroes Viz Selah, Tom, Phillis, Margaret as the property of the Defendant and WF Windle Summoned as guarnishee
D Rushing, Shff, by C Austin DS

State of North Carolina }
Union County }

Mr Wm F Windle Pleas take Notice that on the first Monday in January Next at the Court House in Monroe I Shall Return an attachment before the Justice of the Court of Pleas and Quarter Sessions for said Court wherein Wm G Winchester is Plaintiff and Jonathan B Hart is Defendant when and where you are Summoned to appear as Guarnishee and answer on Certain Relation to what you are indebted to the Defendant and what property and Effects you have in your hands or had at the time of Receiving this Notice belonging to the Defendant and also whether you know of any Debts owing to the Defendant any other persons or any of his Effects Remaining in the hands of any other persons
October the 19th 1850
D Rushing, Shff
By C Austin, DS

****

William Holley Vs. Redden Staton & Jackson Simpson [1850]
Civil Action
Union County

Transcript
Bill Cost
CK.

Writ & Bond	1.40
2 Continuances	.60
Jagk[?] & Bill	1.10
Appl Bond	.60
Tran efut[?] & seal	1.25
	4.95

County Tax	1.00
D Rushing Shff	2.00
Little atty	4.00
	11.95

State of North Carolina }
Union County }

First Monday of October AD 1850 It being the 7th day of the Month. Be it remembered that a Court of Pleas & Quarter Sessions is this day opened and held for the County of Union at the Court house in Monroe.

D.A. Covington, John Blount & Cary Tolson Esqr., Justices appointed by Law to hold said Court Present and presiding.

When a Writ was returned into said Court in the following words and figures "to Wit"

State of North Carolina

To the Sheriff of Union County, Greeting:

You are hereby Commanded to take the bodies of Redden Staton & Jackson Simpson if to be found in your County and them safely Keep so that you have them before the Justices of our Court of Pleas & Quarter sessions at the next Court to be held for the County of Union at the Court house in Monroe on the first Monday of October next then and there to answer William Holley of a Plea that they render unto him the sum of three hundred & six dollars which they owe and injustly detain to his damage one hundred dollars, Herein fail not and have you then and there this writ.

Witness J.M. Stewart Clerk of our said Court at Office, the 1st Monday of July and in the Seventy fourth year of our Independence AD 1850. Issued the 1st day of July 1850.
JM Stewart CCC
Eudorse & as follows thereon viz
William Holley Vs Redden Staton & Jackson Simpson
Writ debt October Term 1850, Executed.
D Rushing, Shff
Little

And it was placed upon the Appearance Docket and Stood as follows to Wit.

Appearance Docket October Term 1850

Debt

Little -- William Holley
3 -- Vs
Osborne -- Redden Staton
Hutchison -- Jackson Simpson

Executed D Rushing, Shff
Specially that the bond declared on was given to Compound a Criminal prosecution, Conto,

From whence it was carried forward and Placed upon the Trial Docket Jany Term 1851. (D.A. Covington, John Blount & Cary Tolson Esq presiding) and stood as follows to wit

---

Trial Docket Jany Term 1851

Debt

Little -- William Holley
17 -- Vs
Osborne -- Redden Staton
Hutchison -- Jackson Simpson

Specially that the bond declared upon was given to Compound a Criminal prosecution, Conto,

From whence it was carried forward and placed upon the Trial Docket Apl Term 1851. D.A. Covington, G.W. May & T.C. Wilson Esqs. presiding and stood as follows.

Trial Docket April Term 1851

Debt

Little -- William Holley

10 -- Vs
Osborne -- Redden Staton
Hutchison -- Jackson Simpson

Specially that the bond declared on was given to Compound a Criminal prosecution

The following Jury Sworn and charged to try the issue viz: AH Griffin, Charles Hagler, William Helms, Coleman Lee, James Mullis, Eleazer Presley, J.W. Harrison, Thos Simpson, Eli Presley, Ambrose Haskey, Jacob L Broom, John Hays.

Who find all Issues in favor of the Plantiff and assess his damage to three hundred and twenty eight Dollars & ninety five cents of Which sum $306.00 dollars is principal money.
Appeal prayed and granted to the next Superior Court. No Security required.

State of North Carolina }
Union County }

I James M. Stewart Clerk do Certify that the foregoing is a true and perfect exemplification of Case William Holley vs Redden Staton & J Simpson and of all the proceeding had therein in said Court.

In testimony Whereof I have hereunto subscribed my name and affixed the seal of said Court at Office in Monroe this 23 Apl 1851.
JM Stewart Clk.

W Holley Vs Redden Staton
Suba for Deft
James Austin, JW Smith, Instanter
Fall Term 1851, Executed on Smith, D Rushing, Shff. I Depute CB Curlie to Execute this Subpoena on J Austin, D Rushing, Shff.

State of North Carolina.
To the Sheriff of Union County, Greeting:
You are hereby commanded to Summon James Austin & JW Smith personally to be and appear before the Judge of our Superior Court,

at the next Court to be held for our said county, at the Court House in Monroe on the 1st Monday, then and there to testify, and the truth to say, in behalf of Deft in a certain matter of controversy before said Court depending, and then and there to be tried, wherein William Holley is Plaintiff, and Redden Staton is defendant. And this shall in no wise omit, under the penalty prescribed by law.

Witness HM Houston Clerk of our said Court, at Office the 1st Monday **[?]** and in the seventy 6th year of our Independence A.D. 1851.
HM Houston Clk

Wm Holley vs Reden Staton
J Simpson
Subpo for Pltff
David Thomas
To Spring Term 1851, Executed, D. Rushing, Shff.

State of North Carolina.
To the Sheriff of Union County, Greeting:

You are hereby commanded to summon David Thomas personally to be and appear before the Judge of our Superior Court of Law, at the next Court to be held for our said County, at the Court House in Monroe on the 6th Monday after 4th Monday in March Instanter, then and there to testify, and the truth to say, in behalf of Plff in a certain matter of controversy before said Court depending, and then and there to be tried, wherein Wm Holley is plaintiff, and R Staton & J Simpson is defendant. And this you shall in no wise omit, under the penalty prescribed by law.

Witness, Wm E. Doster Clerk of our said Court, at Office the 6th Monday after the 4th Monday in March and in the 75 year of our Independence, A.D. 1851.
W.E. Doster Clk.

William Holley
3
Redden Staton, Suba for Deft
John W Smith

to Spring Term 1852
Executed, D Rushing, Shff, By C. Austin, Ds

State of North Carolina.
To the Sheriff of Union County, Greeting:

You are hereby commanded to Summon John W Smith personally to be and appear before the Judge of our Superior Court of Law, at the next Court to be held for our said County, at the Court House in Monroe on the 6th Monday after the 4th Monday in March next, then and there to testify, and the truth to say, in behalf of Deft in a certain matter of controversy before said Court depending, and then and there to be tried, wherein, wherein William Holley is plaintiff, and Redden Staton is defendant. And this you shall in no wise omit, under the penalty prescribed by law.

Witness, HM Houston, Clerk of our said Court, at Office, the 6th Monday after the 4th Monday in Sept and in the seventy 6th year of American Independence, A.D. 1852. Issued 10 March 1852.
HM Houston Clk.

William Holley Vs Redon Staton & Jackson Simpson
Suba for pltf,
To Fall Instanter 1852
not found
D. Rushing, Shff

State of North Carolina.
To the Sheriff of Union County Greeting:

You are hereby commanded to Summon Jackson Simpson personally to be and appear before the Judges of our Superior Court of Law, at the next Court to be held for our said County, at the Court House in Monroe, on the Sixth Monday after the Fourth Monday in September Inst, then and there to testify and the truth to say, in behalf of William Holley in a certain matter of controversy before said Court depending, and then and there to be tried, wherein William Holly is plaintiff, and Redon Staton is defendant. And this you shall in no wise omit, under the penalty prescribed by law.

Witness, HM Houston Clerk of our said Court, at Office, the Sixth Monday after the Fourth Monday in March and in the seventy 6th year of our Independence, A.D. 1852. Issued the 11th day of Novr. 1852. H.M. Houston Clk.

State of North Carolina
To Joshua W Hodges & John M Cochran Esquires, Justices assigned to keep the Peace for the County of Baker and State of Georgia.

Know Ye, that we, reposing special confidence in your fidelity and prudent circumspection, do authorize and empower you, or any of you, that at such time and place as you shall appoint, you call and cause to come before you James A McCollum & others and there diligently examine on the Holy Evangelist of Almighty God, what you may know in and about a matter of controversy, now at issue in our Superior Court of Law for the County of Union wherein William Holley is Plaintiff, and Redden Staton is Defendant, as well on the part of the Plaintiff as the Defendant; and such examination and Deposition by you taken, you are to send, certified and enclosed, under your hands and seals, to the next Court to be held for said County at the Court House in Monroe on the 6th Monday after the 4th Monday in March next; and this you shall in no wise omit.

Witness, HM Houston, Clerk of our said Court, at Office the 6th day of March A.D. 1852, and in the seventy 6th year of our Independence. H.M. Houston Clk.

Clerk of The Superior Court of Union County, N.C.
Committed To the Cear of Josiah Winchester
opened by me HM Houston Clk

State of Georgia }
Baker County } Aprill 22th 1852

We Joshua W Hodges & John M Cochran in pursuance of a Commission to us directed from the Superior Court of Law for the County of Union in the State of North Carolina authorizing and empowering us to take the deposition of James A McCallum in a certain matter of Controversy now at issue in the Superior Court of Law for Union County in the State of North Carolina wherein William Holly is Plaintiff and Redden Staton is Defendant Have caused the said James A McCollum to appear this day before us at the House of the Said James McCollum in the County of Baker and State of Georgia.

Who after being duly Sworn according to Law deposed to the following facts Viz.

Qs. 1st What do you know in and about a matter of Controversy now at issue in the Superior Cort of Law for the County of Union in the State of North Carolina Wherein William Holley is Plaintiff and Redden Staton is defendant.

Ans. I was presant with William Holley and Redden Staton on the Tenth day of January (1850) One thousand Eight Hundred and Fifty at which time Redden Staton gave his note to William Holley for the sum of $306 Three hundred and Six dollars or Thare about.

Qs. 2nd. For what Consideration did Staton give that note to Holley.

Ans. Holley had in his posesion a Negro Man (Ralph) A Slave which Holley allegd. had broken into his House and Stolen Money from him to about that amount and Sed he wood Prosecute the Negro if he did not get his money And Staton gave Holley his Note for that amount of Money in order that the Slave Ralph might not be prosecute for the theft.

Qs. 3rd Who did the Slave Ralph belong to at that time.

Ans. To William Steagall and John McCollum

Qs. 4th Why did Staton interfere with the Slave Ralph.

Ans. It was understood that Stegall and McCollum were boath from home and Staton gave his note and took the Slave Ralph in to his Possession that Holley Might not Prosecute him - as an act of kindness to the owners.

Qs. 5th Have you any Interest directly or Indirectly with the result of this Suite.

Ans. I have not.

Qs 6th Did you not give your note to Staton the Same day for that amount of money and take the Slave Ralph in to Your Possession.

Ans. I Did give Staton my note that day for the Same amount But I have Since received that note and have it in my possession now and have no intrest whatever in the result of Said note Further the deponent Sayeth not.

We hear By certify that the foar going Examination and Deposition of James A McCollum taken by us at his House this day is Corectly Set forth. Witness Our Hands and Seals, April 22 -- 1852.
Joshua W. Hodges, Commissioners (Seal)
John M Cochran, Commissioner (Seal)

John M. Cochran, Commissioner (Seal)
Charles Helms, Commissioner (Seal)

Opened by me HM Houston, Clk

State of North Carolina.
To John M Cochran and Charles Helms, Esquires, Justices assigned to keep the Peace for the County of Baker and State of Georgia.

Know Ye, that we, reposing special confidence in your fidelity and prudent circumspection, do authorize and empower you, or any two of you, that at such time and place as you shall appoint, you call and cause to come before you James A McCollum and him diligently examine on the Holy Evangelist of Almighty God, what he may know in and about a matter of controversy, now at issue in our Superior Court for the County of Union wherein William Holley is Plaintiff, and Redden Staton & Jackson Simpson are Defendants, as well on the part of the Plaintiff as the Defendant; and such examination and Deposition by you taken, you are to send, certified and enclosed, under your hands and seals, to the next Court to be held for said County at the Court House in Monroe on the 1st Monday after 4th Monday Sept next; and this you shall in no wise omit.

Witness, HM Houston Clerk of our said Court, at office the 18th day of May A.D. 1852, and in the seventy Fifth year of our Independence.

H.M. Houston, Clk

W. Holley Vs Redden Staton & Jackson Simpson

State of North Carolina
Union County

This day personally Came JW Smith one of the acting Justices in & for said County Daniel McCollum and maketh oath that he did this day deliver a true copy of the with in to William Holley this the 21st day of May 1852 -- Sworn to & subscribed
Test J.W. Smith
Daniel McCallum

State of North Carolina }
Union County }

W. Holley vs Redden Staton & Jackson Simpson

Mr William Holly Sir please to take notice that on the 10th July 1852 at the dwelling house of James A McCollum in Baker County Georgia I will proceed to take the depositions of James A McCollum & others to be read in evidence in the Case now pending in Union Superior Court W. Holly vs Redden Staton & Jackson Simpson Where you can attend and Cross examine if you think Proper.
Redden Staton

State of Georgia }
Baker County } July the 10th 1852

We John M Cochran and Charles Helms in pursuance of the annexed Commission to us directed from the Superior Court of Law for the County of Union in the State of North Carolina authorising and empowering us to take the deposition of James A McCollum in a certain matter of Controversy now at issue in the Superior Court of Law for Union County in the State of North Carolina Wherein William Holly is

plaintiff and Redin Staton and Jackson Simpson are defendants have this day Caused James A. McCollum to appear before us at the House of the said James A McCollum in Baker County in the State of Georgia who after being duty sworn according to law Deposeth as follows:
William Holly Vs Redin Staton & Jackson Simpson

Qs. 1st What do you know in and about the matter of controversy above stated.

Ans. I was present with William Holly, Redin Staton and Jackson Simpson on the 10th day of January 1850 when Redin Staton gave his Note with Jackson Simpson security to William Holly for three hundred and six dollars or there about.

Qs. 2nd For what consideration did Staton give that Note to Holly.

Ans. Holly had in his possession a Negro man Ralph which he (Holly) alledged had stolen money from him to that amount or there about and said that he would posecute the Negro if he did not get his money and Staton gave his Note with Jackson Simpson as security to Holly for that amount of money in order that the slave Ralph might not be prosecuted.

Qs. 3rd Who did the Negro belong to at that time.

Ans. It was understood that he belonged to Wm Stegall and John McCollum.

Qs. 4th Why did Staton interfere with the matter.

Ans. It was understood that Stegall and McCollum were both from home and Staton gave his Note to William Holly and took the Negro into his possession as an act of kindness to the owners.

Qs. 5th Have you any interests directly or indirectly with the result of this Suit.

Ans. I have not.

Qs. 6th Did you not give your Note to Staton the same day for the same amount of Money and take the Slave Ralph into your possession.

Ans. I did. But I have since received that Note and have it now in my possession and have no interests whatever in the result of the pending Suit.

Further the Deponent Saith not
We John M Cochran and Charles Helms hereby certify that the foregoing Examination and Deposition of James A. McCollum taken by us at his house this the 10th day of July 1852 is correctly set forth.

In witness whereof we hereunto Set our hands and Seals, date above.
Charles Helms (Seal
John M Cochran (Seal)

Wm Holley Vs Redden Staton
Subpoena for Pltff
Jackson Simpson
To Spring term 1853, Executed, D. Rushing, Shff, By C Austin, Ds

State of North Carolina.
To the Sheriff of union County, Greeting:

You are hereby commanded to Summon Jackson Simpson personally to be and appear before the Judges of our Superior Court of Law, at the next Court to be held for our said County, at the Court House in Monroe, on the Sixth Monday after the Fourth Monday in March next, then and there to testify and the truth to say, in behalf of Wm Holley in a certain matter of controversy before said Court depending, and then and there to be tried, wherein William Holley is plaintiff, and Redden Staton is defendant. and this you shall in no wise omit, under the penalty prescribed by law.

Witness, HM Houston Clerk of our said Court, at Office, the Sixth Monday after the Fourth Monday in September and in the seventy [?] year of our Independence, A.D. 1853. Issued the 13th day of January 1853.
H.M. Houston CSC

****

J.A. McNeely Vs. M.M. Chaney [1855]
Civil Action
Union County

State of North Carolina }
Union County }

J.A. McNeely maketh oath before me JM Stewart Clerk of the Court of Pleas & Quarter Sessions of the County & State aforesaid that M.M. Chaney is justly indebted to him in the Sum of three hundred and twenty two dollars & thirty four cents ($322.34) to the best of his Knowledge & belief, and that the said M.M. Chaney so absconds or conceals himself that the Ordinary process of the law cannot be served on him. JA McNeely
Sworn to & subscribed before me this 17th day of October AD 1855
JM Stewart CCC
J.T. Hough DC

State of North Carolina }
Union County }

To the Sheriff of Union County, Whereas J.A. McNeely hath complained on oath before me JM Stewart Clerk of our Court of Pleas & Quarter Sessions of Union County that M.M. Chaney is justly indebted to him in the sum of three hundred & twenty two Dollars and thirty four cents, and oath having been also made that the said MM Chaney so absconded or conceals himself that the ordinary process of the law Cannot be served on him and the said J.A. McNeely having given bond & security according to law. we therefore command you, that you attach the Estate of the said M.M. Chaney to be found in your County or so much thereof replevable on security as shall be of value Sufficient to satisfy the said debt & costs according to the complaint, and such estate so attached in your hands to secure or so to provide that the same may be liable to further proceedings thereupon to be had at the Court of Pleas & Quarter Sessions to be held at the Court House in Monroe on the first Monday in January next so as to compel the said M.M. Chaney to appear and answer the above complaint of the said JA McNeely when & where you shall make known how you have executed this writ.

Witness JM Stewart Clerk of said Court at office in Monroe the seventeenth day of Oct. AD 1855 in the 80th year of our Independence.
JM Stewart Clk
J.F. Hough DC

State of North Carolina }
Union County }

Know all men by these presents that we JA McNeely & W.S. Howie are held & firmly bound unto MM Chaney in the in the Sum of six hundred & forty four 68/100 Dollars to be paid to him his certain Attorney, executors, administrators or assigns for which payment well and truly to be made we bind ourselves our heirs, executors & administrators, jointly & severally sealed with our seals & dated this 17th day of Oct. AD 1855.

The Condition of the above obligation is such that whereas the above bound JA McNeely hath this day prayed an attachment in his favor against the Estate of the above named MM Chaney for the sum of three hundred & twenty two dollars and thirty four cents and hath obtained the same returnable to the next Court of Pleas and Quarter Sessions to be held for the County of Union at the Court House in Monroe on the first Monday in January next.

Now if the said Plaintiff shall prosecute his said suit with effect or in case he fail therein shall well & truly pay & satisfy to the said defendant all such costs & damages as shall be awarded & recovered against the said Plaintiff, his heirs, executors or administrators in any Suit or Suits which may be hereafter brought for wrongfully suing out the said attachment, then the above obligation to be void, otherwise to remain in full force & effect.

Test J.F. Hough JA McNeely (Seal)
W.L. Howie (Seal)

October the 17th 1855
I deputise Robt. S Huntly to Execute the within

J Sikes, Shff

5 o'clock the 17th Oct 1855
This atachment this our Executed by leving on one negro Woman naimd Ann the property of MM Chaney.
J Sikes, Shff
by R.S. Huntly, DS

****

Gilbert Grace & Wife Vs. John Marsh [1859]
Civil Action
Union County

Eliza Grace
Petition to Sue
in Forma Pauperis

To the Honorable Robert Heath one of the Judges of the Judges of the Superior Court of Law & Equity for the State of North Carolina.

The Humble Petition of Eliza Grace sheweth that some years since viz about the year 1856 her brother Joseph Faulkner now dead, held a negro woman named Clara in trust for her sole and separate use, and that about two or three years ago, her trustee the said Joseph Faulkner sold the said negro to one Parks Bumas[?] of Anson County -- that she has not yet brought an action for said negro, being unable to give security for the prosecution of the said Suit and to carry on the said Cause by reason of her extreme poverty. Your Petitioner therefore prays your Honor that she may be admitted to prosecute her said Suit in Equity in forma pauperis in the name of herself and her husband Gilbert Grace against the said Parks Bumas[?] and such other persons as it may be deemed necessary to make parties defendants with him and that Messrs Ashe & Hargrove may be assigned to her as Counsel to prosecute.
Eliza Grace
We Humbly conceive from the statement of her case made to me by the Petitioner that she has good cause of action and cannot [?] her counsel.
Ashe & Hargrove

North Carolina }
Anson County }

Eliza Faulkner makes oath that her husband is insolvent and that she is not worth five pounds in the world save and except a tract of land of fifty two acres lying in Anson County which has been reserved to her separate use in fee simple if she survives her husband but if her husband survives, then after her death to her children which land is not in her possession or within her control, the same **[Faded]** been taken possession of by one Joseph White as she is informed and believes, and rented out by him, whether in his own right or as Executor of Joseph Faulkner her late Trustee, she does not know, and except her claims to the negro in continuum and another similarly situation for which she will have to bring Suit, and except some dues for **[Faded]** in the hands of J White which he refuses to pay her.
Eliza Grace

Sworn to and Subscribed before me this 29th day of October AD 1859.
In testimony whereof I Robert T Hall Clerk of the Superior Court have hereunto affixed the Seal of said Court at office in Wadesborough this 29th October AD 1859
Robert T Hall CSC

State of North Carolina

Upon reading the Petition and affidavit of Eliza Grace and the certificate of Counsel I admit the Plaintiff Eliza Grace to sue in her own and husbands names, in forma pauperis in the Court of Equity for the County of Anson and I do hereby assign to her Thomas T Ashe and JR Hargrove to be her Counsel. The Clerk & Master of said Court is hereby ordered to issue copies of a bill in Equity and the necessary subpoenas and other process in favor of the said Eliza Grace, suing in her own and her husband Gilbert Graces names against Parks Bumas[?] and any other person or persons her Counsel herein assigned to her may deem advisable to make parties defendants, when applying for without requiring any surety for the prosecution

Nov 4, 1859
R.R. Heath
J.S.C. & E

Gilbert Grace & Wife Vs John Marsh
O.B.
To Spring Term 1860
Ashe Sol.

State of North Carolina } In Equity
Union County } Spring Term 1860

To the Honorable the Judge of Said Court

The Bill of Complaint of Gilbert Grace and wife Eliza Grace Against John Marsh.

Humbly Complaining, Showeth to your Honor, your Orator and Oratrix, that about the 10th day of July 1850, Susan Falkner, of the County of Anson, in the State aforesaid, who is the Mother of your Oratrix, executed a deed of conveyance to George W Little of Said last named County, therein Conveying to said GW Little two negroes Viz Clara & Abram, in trust for the Sole and Separate use of your Oratrix a copy of which is hereto annexed & prayed to be taken as part of this bill who is the wife of your Oratrix Gilbert. That at Term 185**[Blank]** of the Court of Equity for Anson County, a decree was obtained, upon the petition of your Oratrix, removing the Said GW Little from his Said Office of Trustee and Appointing & Substituting in his Place as Trustee, Joseph W Falkner, Late of said County of Anson, who accepted the same, and as such received into his possession from said George W. Little the negro woman Clara and her child Jim (who was born the year after said deed was executed), Said negro Abram being previously Sold by Said GW Little under a decree of the Court of Equity for Anson; That Shortly after Said JW Falkner was appointed trustee, your Oratrix became desirous of Selling Said Negroes Clara & Jim for the purpose of investing the proceeds in land under the Same trusts, and thereupon Said JW Falkner had Said negroes valued by some disinterested persons, & Said he would take them himself at the valuation, and in lieu of them that he would Convey to your Oratrix, or by proper Conveyances Substitute a Certain tract of land Situate in Anson County which Said JW Falkner then owned, in the place of Said negroes & to be held under the Same Trusts; and upon that Condition Your Oratrix assented to his taking Said negroes. Your Orator and Oratrix further Shows that about a year after Said valuations was made, Said J.W. Falkner took the negroes Clara & Jim into his actual possession, (they having previously been in the possession of your Orator & Oratrix, and Some time in the year 1855 or 1856 Sold said negro Jim to the Defendant John Marsh, without any authority either from your Oratrix or the Court of Equity, And without your Oratrix's Consent, and applied the proceeds of Said Sale to his Own Use; Your Oratrix further shows that Said JW Falkner never did Comply with his agreement with her, by having Said land Substituted, under Said trust in place of the negroes, but that on the Contrary, Since that time he has Sold and Conveyed Said land absolutely to Joseph White of Anson County; & received the proceeds thereof to his Own use; She further Shows that Said JW Falkner has since to wit in October 1858, died leaving a last will & testament therein appointing Said Joseph White Executor, that the Same has been admitted to probate in Anson County Court, & Said Executor duly qualified thereto.

Your Orator And Oratrix Charge that the defendant, at the time he purchased the negro Jim read notice of the trust under which Said Falkner held said negro & that Said deed from Susan Falkner to Geo W Little was duly proven & registered in the Registers Office of Anson County; that Said negro Jim is now worth eight hundred dollars as she is informed and believes & that she has demanded the Surrender of Said negro from the defendant Marsh, which he refused And inasmuch as your Oratrix is without remedy, in the premises , except in this Honorable Court. Your Oratrix prays that the defendant may be declared, by a decree of this Court, to hold Said negro Jim in trust under the same limitations he was held by Said JW Falkner, and that Said defendant may be Compelled by a decree of this Court to convey & Surrender Said negro to your Oratrix or some other Suitable person for her use and benefit, and on failure So to do, to Account to your Oratrix for the value of Said negro and that he may be required also to account to your Oratrix for the hire of Said negro Since he has been in his possession; and to that end, that all proper & necessary accounts may be taken, under the direction of this Court, and your Oratrix prays for such other & further relief in the premises as to your Honor shall seem right & proper. Your Oratrix prays your Honor that the States writ of Subpoena with a copy of this bill, be issued to the defendant John Marsh, summoning him to be & appear at

the next Term of this Court to be held at the Court House in Monroe, then & there to plead answer or demur to said bill -- and your Orator & Oratrix, as in duty bound will ever pray.
Thos. S. Ashe, Sol.

State of North Carolina }
Anson County }

Eliza Grace makes oath before me that the several matters & things Setforth in the foregoing bill as of her own Knowledge are true, and those not so Stated She believes to be true.
Eliza Grace

Sworn to Subscribed before me Robert T Hall Clerk of the Superior Court for Anson County. In testimony whereof I have hereunto affixed the Seal of Said Court on this 7th day of November 1859.
Robert T Hall CSC

Susan Falkner to GW Little
Deed of Trust, Copy

State of North Carolina }
Anson County }

This Indenture made this 17 day of October 1850 between Susan Faulkner of the County of Anson and State of North Carolina of the one part and George W Little of the County and State aforesaid of the other part, Witnesseth that the said Susan Faulkner for and in consideration of the sum of five dollars to her in hand paid by the said George W Little hath sold and by these presents doth bargain and sell unto the said George W Little his Executors and administrators for purposes and under restrictions hereinafter mentioned two negro slaves to wit, a negro woman by the name of Clara about 38 years of age and a boy by the name of Abram about thirteen years of age the conditions and limitations are such that being desirous of rendering some assistance to her daughter Eliza Grace and for the consideration before mentioned the said negroes are hereby conveyed to the said George W Little [?] by him held in trust for the sole and separate use and benefit of the said Eliza Grace separate and apart from her husband Gilbert Grace and not having in any wise to be liable to the contracts or debts of said Gilbert but the said Eliza to enjoy their services ot the amount of their hire free and clear from all liability for her said husbands contracts not including to hold the said George W Little in any way for the acts of others. Witness my hand and seal Oct. 17 1850 Susan Faulkner

Witness A Myers

State of North Carolina } October Term 1859
Anson County }

Then the Execution of this land was duly proven in open Court by A Myers and ordered to be registered
ND Boggan Clerk

State of North Carolina }
Anson County }

I, EF Kendall, Public Register for Anson County do hereby Certify the above to be a true and correct Copy of a Deed of Trust made by Susan Falkner to George W Little as Recorded in the Registers office of Anson County in Book 13 page 312.
E.F. Kendall Public Register.

Gilbert Grace & Wife Vs John Marsh
Writ Subpoena
Spring Term 1860
April the 21st 1860
Executed by delivering a Copy of the original Bill & the deed of Trust
C Austin Shff

State of North Carolina.
To the Sheriff of Union County, Greeting:

You are hereby commanded to summon John Marsh personally to be and appear before the Judge of the Court of Equity at the next Court to be held for our said County, at the Court House in Monroe on the 10th Monday after the 4th Monday in February next, then and there to Answer the several alegations of a Bill of Complaint before said Court depending, and then and there to be tried, wherein Gilbert Grace & Wife Eliza Grace is Plaintiff, and John Marsh is Defendant. And this you shall in no wise omit, under the penalty prescribed by law.

Witness, TD Winchester Clerk of our said Court at Office the 10th Monday in August, and in the 84th year of our Independence, Anno Domini 1859. Issued the 23rd day of March 1860
T.D. Winchester CME

Gilbert Grace & Wife Vs John S Marsh
Answer of the defendant Jno. S. Marsh
To Spring Term 1860
In Equity, Union County
Lander Atto

North Carolina }In Equity
Union County } To Spring Term 1860

To the Honorable the Judge of the Said Court

The Answer of John S Marsh, to the bill of Complaint of Gilbert Grace & Wife Eliza Grace filed against this defendant in the said Court. This defendant Now & at all times hereafter Saving and reserving to himself all and all Manner of benefit of exceptions, which Can or Maybe had or taken to the many errors, uncertainties, inconsistencies, and false statements, in said Complaints said bill of Complaint contained for answer thereunto or unto so much thereof as he this defendant is advised is material & necessary for him to Make answer unto, he this defendant answereth & Saith that it is true that he this defendant purchased a certain negro boy Named Jim from JW Falkner, at the price of five hundred dollars, and this defendant shows that he paid a full and fair price for said negro, at the time of the purchase, the negro boy then being only about five years old, this defendant further Shows that he purchased the said slave on the 2d day of April 1857, this defendant answering further denies that he had any Notice whatever of any Equity of Complainants, or either of them - on the Contrary he avers the facts to be, as follows to wit, After the making of the deed, and the appointment of J.W. Faulkner to be trustee instead of George W. Little - all which facts this respondent believes are correctly set forth in Complainants bill -- the Complainants - and particularly the Complainant Eliza, became desirous of having the negroes conveyed to the use of the said Eliza sold, and the proceeds invested in a tract of land to be held by the said Faulkner on the same trusts and they requested the trustee Faulkner that he would sell the negroes and so invest the proceeds, the said Faulkner was a near relative of Complainant Eliza, and being desirous of applying the trust estate in the manner most beneficial to her, he acceded to her Said request and proceeded before Selling Said negroes to have them valued by competent disinterested Persons, the said Negroes were so valued but the valuation fixed upon them was so high that Faulkner was unable to sell them for the Price, he then, being anxious on account of his relationship to said Eliza to do all in his Power for her accommodation at her request agreed to take the Negroes and advance the survey for the Purchase of the land, he accordingly contracted with one **[Blank]** for the Purchase of a tract of land, that Complainants went to reside on said tract of land, that Faulkner advanced to said Eliza the sum of three hundred dollars in Stocking said Plantation for which he took her receipt -- which receipt is now in the hands of Joseph White Executor of said Faulkner who is since deceased -- that before the deed for said land was made according to the terms of the agreement aforesaid to the use of said Eliza, the Complainants & especially Eliza, became desirous of returning to the State of Mississippi and requested the trustee to sell said land and advance to the said Eliza the trust fund in order to assist them to commence the World**[?]** in their new home, the said Faulkner being now desirous of assisting his relative, than careful to Protect his own interest acceeded to this request, and at that time to wit in the year 1848 advanced to Complainant Eliza the Sum of Six hundred & fifty five dollars & 82 cents which sum as respondent is informed and believes covered the Whole amount of the trust fund in his hands, and took her note for that amount, expressing in the face that it should be paid out of the separate estate of said Eliza, which Note is as Respondent is informed & believes is now in the possession of the executor of the said Faulkner & is still due and unpaid.

Further answering respondent showeth unto your Honor that at the time he Purchased said Slave in the Pleadings mentioned, Complainants were residing on the land so Purchased for the use of Complainant Eliza, & enjoying the Personal estate so Purchased for her use; and respondent supposed that the agreement made between the Complainants & Said Faulkner had been fully carried out, and further that Complainants at no time to the knowledge of respondent set up any Claim to the Slave Jim until after the death of the trustee Faulkner, Further answering respondent Submits that Joseph White Executor of J.W. Faulkner deceased is a necessary Party to this Suit, in order that all Matters in Controversy & all interested Parties may be heard by the Court.

Further answering this defendant again denies that JW Faulkner sold said Negro Jim to this defendant contrary to the will and consent of Complainant Eliza Grace, but on the contrary alleges, that the whole transaction was performed at her special instance and request; This defendant also denies that said JW Faulkner, applied the proceeds of the Sale of said Negro Jim to his own use, but on the contrary charges that said JW faulkner appropriated all the Money for the use and benefit of Complainant Eliza Grace and according to her request and desire.

This defendant Again denies that he at the time he Purchased said Negro from JW Faulkner had any Notice of the trusts under which Faulkner held said Slave, but on the contrary this defendant fully believed at the time he Purchased the said Slave Jim that said J.W. Faulkner owned the said Slave absolutely as his own Property free and discharged from all equities and trusts of any and every kind whatsoever;

This defendant shows further that JW Falkner is now dead and his estate is insolvent.

Further answering this defendant shows that the bill of Sale under he purchased said Slave from JW Falkner is in the following wordss & figures to wit Received of Jno. S Marsh five hundred dollars in full payment for a negro boy Named Jim about five years of Age, the right & title of Said Slave I warrant and defend against the Claims of any and all persons whatsoever, and warrant him sound and healthy, April 2d 1857.
Witness JW Falkner (Seal)
Simeon Marsh

This defendant further answering denies all part and having fully answered prays to be dismissed with his reasonable Cost in this behalf Most unjustly expending.
Lander, Atto

John S Marsh the defendant in this Cause Makes Oath that the Matters & facts as set forth in the foregoing answer are of his own knowledge are true and those as not of his own knowledge he believes to be.

****

John D. Stewart Vs. George F. Howie [1855]
Civil Action
Union County

John D Stewart Vs G.F. Howie
Original attachmt.
To October Term 1855

State of North Carolina }
Union County }

John D. Stewart maketh oath before me G.M. Stewart, Clerk of the Court of Pleas & Quarter Sessions of the County & State aforesaid that George Franklin Howey is justly indebted to him in the Sum of Two hundred & three 48/100 dollars ($203.48) to the best of his knowledge & belief; and that the said George Franklin Howey, so absconds or conceals himself, or is an inhabitant of another State, that the ordinary process of the law cannot be served on him.
John D Stewart
Sworn to & Subscribed before me this 6th day of August A.D. 1855.
JM Stewart, Clerk

State of North Carolina }
Union County }

To the Sheriff of Union County, Greeting:

Whereas John D. Stewart hath complained on oath before J. M. Stewart Clerk of our Court of Pleas & Quarter Sessions of Union County, that George F. Howey is justly indebted to him in the sum of Two hundred & three 48/100 dollars & oath having also been made that the said George F. Howey hath removed himself out of Your County or so absconds or conceals himself that the ordinary process of the law cannot be served on him, & the said John D. Stewart having given bond & Security according to law; We therefore Command You that you attach the estate of the said George F. Howey to be found in Your County, or so much thereof repleviable on Security, as shall be of value Sufficient to Satisfy the said debt & Costs according to the complaint; & such estate so attached, in your hands to secure, or so to provide that the same may be liable to further proceedings thereupon, to be had at the Court of Pleas & Quarter Sessions to be held at the Court house in the town of Monroe in the County of Union & State aforesaid on the first Monday in October next, so as to compel the said George F. Howey, to appear & answer the above complaint of the said John D. Stewart, when & where you shall make known to the said Court how you shall have executed this writ.

Witness J.M. Stewart Clerk of said Court at office in Monroe, the first Monday in July AD 1855, and in the year of our Independence the 79. Issued the 6th day of Augt. 1855.

State of North Carolina }
Union County }

Know all men by these presents that we John D Stewart & Hugh M. Houston both of Union County are held & firmly bound unto George F. Howey in the Sum of Four hundred & Six 96/100 dollars to be paid to him, his certain attorney, Executors and Administrators, jointly & Severally, Sealed with our Seals & dated this 6th day of August A.D. 1855.

The Condition of the above obligation is such that whereas the above bounden John D. Stewart hath this day prayed an attachment in his favour, against the estate of the above named George F. Howey for the sum of Two hundred & three 48/100 dollars & interest on the same from January last & hath obtained the same returnable to the Next Court of Pleas & Quarter Sessions to be held for the County of Union at the Court house in Monroe on the first Monday in October next. Now if the Said John D Stewart plaintiff shall prosecute his Said Suit with effect, or in Case he fail therein, shall well & truly pay & satisfy to the said defendant all such costs & damages as shall be awarded & recovered against the said John D. Stewart plaintiff, his heirs executors or administrators in any Suit or Suits which may be hereafter brought for wrongfully suing out the said

Attachment then the above obligation to be void, otherwise to remain in full force & effect.
John D. Stewart (Seal)
H.M. Houston (Seal)

The within Attachment is this day executed by levying on One Negroe Slave as the Property of the defendant Named Charles and Confining him in the Common Jail of Union this 6th August 1855.
J Sikes, Shff

****

Needham Armfield Vs. David Moore & James Moore [1849]
Civil Action
Union County

Needham Armfield Vs David Moore & James Moore
Replevin
To Fall Term 1849
Executed and Bond, filed D. Rushing, Shff

State of North Carolina }
Union County }

This day, Needham Armfield personally appeared before me, Joseph T. Draffin, Clerk of the Superior Court for the County and State aforesaid, and made Oath, That within the last Twelve months he was in possession of two Negroes, [?] named Peny aged about Twenty Seven, of the value of Five Hundred Dollars and her child Amanda, aged about one year, of the value of One Hundred & fifty Dollars, and that he has been deprived of the possession of said Negroes, by David Moore and James Moore, without his consent or permission -- Sworn to and subscribed before me, this the 4th day of October A.D. 1849
N Armfield
JT Draffin CC

North Carolina }

Union County }

Know all men by these presents That We Needham Armfield as principal and Hugh M Houston as Security are held and firmly bound unto David Moore and James Moore in the penal sum of thirteen Hundred Dollars, to be void on Condition that sd. Armfield stands to, abides by, and performs **[?]** final Judgment as may be Awarded against him in an action of Replevin this day brought by sd. Armfield against David Moore and James Moore for the recovery of Two Negroes named Peny & her child Amanda, which Suit has been brought to Union Superior Court -- In Witness whereof we have hereunto set our hands and affixed our Seals, this the 4th day of October A.D. 1849.

N. Armfield (Seal)
H.M. Houston (Seal)
JT Draffin

North Carolina }
Union County }

To the Sheriff of Union County, greeting:

Whereas Needham Armfield hath Complained upon Oath before me that he was po**[Torn]** within the last **[Torn]** **[Faded]**uths of two **[Torn]**, one named Peny aged about Twenty Seven years of the value of Five Hundred dollars, and her child Amanda aged about one year of the value of One Hundred & fifty Dollars and that he has been deprived of such possession by David Moore and James Moore of the County aforesaid, without his permission or consent.

And Whereas the Sd. Needham Armfield has given Bond with Hugh Houston as Security in conformity to Law in the Sum of Thirteen Hundred Dollars, being double the value of the Slaves aforesaid, pay**[?]** to the Sd. David Moore and James Moore and Conditional to stand to, abide by, and perform the final Judgment of the Court.

You are therefore hereby commandedto seize and forthwith to take into your custody ans possession the Sd. Negro Slaves Peny and her child Amanda, and deliver them to the said Needham Armfield, the Plaintiff in this Suit, unless the Sd. David Moore and James Moore shall Execute and deliver to you a Bond with approved Security in double the

amount of the sworn value of Sd. Slaves herein described payable to the Sd. Needham Armfield conditional to Stand to, abide by & perform such final Judgment **[Torn]** may be so**[Torn]** **[Torn]** against them **[Torn]** Sd. David Moore & James Moore **[Torn]** the final determination of this Suit, And have you this Writ with the proceedings thereon returnable before the Judge of our next Superior Court of Law to be held for County aforesaid at the Court House in Monroe on the 6th Monday after the 4th Monday in september 1849, Herein fail not -- Witness Joseph T. Draffin Clerk of our said Court, at Office, this the 6th Monday after the 4th Monday in March 1849 and in the 73d Year of American Independence A.D. 1849.
Issued October the 4th 1849
J T Draffin CSC

****

Joseph Blair Vs. James Marsh [1852]
Civil Action
Union County

Joseph Blair vs James Marsh
Writ Covenant
Damages $600
To Spring Term 1852
Executed, D. Rushing, Shff

State of North Carolina.
To the Sheriff of Union County, Greeting:

You are hereby commanded to take the body of James Marsh if to be found in your County, and him safely keep, so that you have him before the Judge of our Superior Court of Law, at the next Court to be held for the County of Union at the Court House in Monroe on the sixth Monday after the fourth Monday in March next, then and there to answer Joseph Blair of a plea of Covenants broken & not performed to his damage Six hundred dollars. Herein fail not; and have you then and there this writ.

Witness, HM Houston Clerk of our said Court, at Office, the Sixth Monday after the 4th Monday in September 1851, and in the seventy fifth year of our Independence, A.D. 1851. Issued the 3rd day of November 1851.

HM Houston, Clk

Notice to James Marsh
Executed by Delivering a Copy of this Notice at the Residence of James Marsh May the 26th 1852. D. Rushing, Shff

State of North Carolina
Union County
Joseph Blair vs James Marsh

Mr. James Marsh Sir please to take Notice that on the 7th day of June at the dwelling house of Lord H Blair in Mecklenburg County N. Carolina & will proceed to take the deposition of Lord H Blair to be read as evidence in the Case now pending in Union Superior Court, Joseph Blair vs James Marsh When you Can attend and Cross examine if you think proper.
Joseph Blair.

State of North Carolina.
To Jos Hall and AJ Hood
Esquires, Justices assigned to keep the Peace for the County of Mecklenburg and State of North Carolina

[The first line of this document is missing]
circumspection, do authorize and empower you, or any two of you, that at such time and place as you shall appoint, you call and cause to come before you Lord H. Blair and him diligently examine on the Holy Evangelist of Almighty God, what he may know in and about a matter of controversy; now at issue in our Superior Court of Law for the County of Union wherein Joseph Blair is Plaintiff, and James Marsh is Defendant, as well on the part of the Plaintiff as the Defendant; and such examination and Deposition by you taken, you are to send, certified and enclosed, under your hands and seals, to the next Court to be held for said county at the Court House in Monroe on the 6th Monday after the 4th Monday in Sept. next; and this you shall in no wise omit.

Witness H.M. Houston Clerk of our said Court, at Office the 5th day of June A.D. 1852, and in the seventy 6th year of our Independence.

H.M. Houston CSC

State of North Carolina
Mecklenburg County, June 7, 1852

A Deposision of Lord H Blair for to be red as Evidence in Monroe in a Suit Depending With Joseph Blair as Plaintiff and James Marsh is Defendant Consarning a Negroe

Question first By the Plantif: are you a Sutscriben Witnes to this Bill of Sail? answer: I am, Dou you Now a Negroe By the Name of Lord Named in that Bill of Sail: anser **[Torn and creased]** Sum of Lord, Ans.: it was three Hundred or three Hundred and fifty Dollers. Quest. Do you now the Sum given for all the Negroes Named in this Bill of Sail. Ans. I do. It was Eleven Hundred and fifty Dollars. Quest. Was that amount a Sufficient Sum at that time for them Negroes. Ans. It Was. Quest. About that time and from that on Did you now Lord to Be Sound. Ans. I Nowd Him not to Be Sound. Quest. When Did you See the first Simpsoms of Him Not Beeing Sound. Ans. the Day that he Was Baught I Saw Him Beeing Short of Breth and was asked What Was the Matter with Him He said it was a pain in his Brest or the Cramp Chalick I have Saw Him at Diferents Times When he Was a Chasing git aut of Breth and fall or if He Would go Whare Thare Was Smoak Be Short of Breth and Complaind of that pain. Quest. Did you ever Notice any Cough on Him. Ans. I have, he hed a Short Caugh. Quest. You have Nowen that Negroe Ever Sence I Baught him, What would you Consider that Negro was Worth to Me. Ans. I had Consider him Worth Nothing to Now Body. Quest. Did you and Mr Marsh Ever have any Conversation about the Soundness of them Negroes. Ans. Mr Marsh Said Lord would Talk Work off & said He Complaind of Having the Cramp a Littel Som Time.

Defendant
Quest. How Long Did you Stay in Union County after I Sold these Negroes. Ans. I Staid till I Maid two Crops. Quest. Did this Negroe Lord go back and forward to the Brown Creek place with the other hands. Ans. He Went When He Was able and When He Was not he dident. Quest. How far from Home was that plaice. Ans. it Was 8 or Nine

Miles. Quest. Dident Mr. Blair frequently Travel that Road in the Night. Ans. Some Times he Did. Quest. How Long after Mr. Blair Bought these Negroes was It that Lord was taken Down with the fevor. Ans. It was not More than one or Two Months till He Was Taking Down I Cant Say it was a fevar or What. Quest. Did you Not Tell Thomas Huntly that that negro Was Down With the fevor. Ans. I Did Not as I Ever Recolect of. LH Blair (SS)

Test Jas Hall, JP
Test AJ Hood, JP

Joseph Blair vs James Marsh
afft
May Term 1852, heard & granted

Joseph Blair } Superior Court of Law
vs } Fall Term 1852
James Marsh }

The Plaintiff maketh oath that said H Blair is in a Low State of health and that it is doubtful whether said LH Blair will live, to testify in this Case, he prays to be permitted to take the deposition of Said Lord H Blair to be read as evidence in this Case on giving to the defendant such notice as your Honor shall deem proper, and that such deposition be taken at Said Lord H Blair's own house, He also maketh oath that Docr Richard E Wiley will be a material witness for him in the Trial of this Cause that said Witness resides in the District of Lancaster South Carolina which adjoins this County and prays for an order to take his depositions in this Case to be read as evidence an giving the Defendant Twenty days notice, said deposition to be taken at Lancaster C House, a distance of about thirty miles from this place, and also that Samuel Carter will be a material witness for him in this Case, that said Witness resides in Chesterfield District So. Ca. about 19 miles from this place and prays for an order to take his deposition at said Carters house on giving Twenty days notice thereof -- Sworn to & Subscribed before me 4 May 1852.
Joseph Blair

HM Houston, Clk

Ordered that the plaintiff have permission to take the deposition of Lord H Blair as prayed for on giving Ten days notice & that the prayer of the affiant is **[?]** respectfuly be granted.

Jos. Blair vs Jas Marsh
Notice Executed by Delivering a Copy of this Notice to James Marsh the 8th of Oct. 1852, D. Rushing, Shff

State of North Carolina
Union County
Jos. Blair vs James Marsh

Mr James Marsh Sir Take Notice that on the 1st day of November next at the Court House in Lancaster District South Carolina I shall take the Deposition of RE Wiley to be read as evidence in the Suite Wherein I am Plaintiff and you are Defendant Now pending for Trial in the Superior Court of Union County When you may attend and cross Examine if you think proper this the 4th Sept 1852.
Joseph Blair

State of North Carolina
To John Williams Esq Magistrate, Lancaster District, Esquires, Justices assigned to keep the Peace for the County of **[Blank]** and State of **[Blank].**

Know ye, that we reposing special confidence in your fidelity and prudent circumspection, do authorize and empower you, or any of you, that at such time and place as you shall appoint, you call and cause to come before you Dr Richard E Wylie and him diligently examine on the Holy Evangelist of Almighty God, what he may know in and about a matter of controversy, now at issue in our Superior Court for the County of Union wherein Joseph Blair is Plaintiff, and James Marsh is Defendant as well on the part of the Plaintiff as the Defendant; and such examination and Deposition by you taken, you are to send, certified and enclosed, under your hands and seals, to the next Court to be held for said County at the Court House in Monroe on the 6th Monday after the 4th Monday in September next; and this you shall in no wise omit.

Witness HM Houston Clerk of our said Court, at office the 6th day of May A.D. 1852.
H.M. Houston CSC

Joseph Blair vs James Marsh
Subp for Pltff
W. McHouston
To Fall Term 1852
Executed, TN Alexander, Shff, by Hovis[?], DS
to hand 25th August 1852

State of North Carolina.
To the Sheriff of Mecklenburg County, Greeting:

You are hereby commanded to Summon William McHouston personally to be and appear before the Judges of our Superior Court of Law, at the next Court to be held for our said County, at the Court House in Monroe on the 6th Monday after the 4th Monday in September next, then and there to testify and the truth to say, in behalf of Joseph Blair in a certain matter of controversy before said Court depending, and then and there to be tried, wherein Joseph Blair is plaintiff, and James Marsh is defendant. And this you shall in no wise omit, under the penalty prescribed by law.

Witness, HM Houston Clerk of our said Court, at Office the 6th Monday after the 4th Monday in March, and in the seventy 6th year of our Independence, A.D. 1852.
H.M. Houston CSC

Joseph Blair vs James Marsh
Subpoena for Dft.
A Lewallen
To Fall Term, 1852
Executed, D. Rushing, Shff

State of North Carolina.
To the Sheriff of Union County, Greeting:

You are hereby commanded to Summon A. Lewallen personally to be and appear before the Judges of our Superior Court of Law, at the next Court to be held for our said County, at the Court House in Monroe on the 6th Monday after the 4th Monday in September next, then and there to testify and the truth to say, in behalf of James Marsh in a certain matter of controversy before said Court depending, and then and there to be tried, wherein Joseph Blair is plaintiff, and James Marsh is defendant. And this you shall in no wise omit, under the penalty prescribed by law.

Witness, HM Houston, Clerk of our said Court, at Office the 6th Monday after the 4th Monday in March and in the seventy 6th year of our Independence, A.D. 1852. Issued Oct. 14th, 1852.
H.M. Houston Clk

Joseph Blair Vs James Marsh
Subpoena for Deft.
John Elliot
To Fall Term, 1852
Executed, D. Rushing, Shff

State of North Carolina.
To the Sheriff of Union County, Greeting:

You are hereby commanded to Summon John Elliot personally to be and appear before the Judges of our Superior Court of Law, at the next Court to be held for our said county, at the Court House in Monroe on the 6th Monday after the 4th Monday in September next, then and there to testify and the truth to say, in behalf of James Marsh in a certain matter of controversy before said Court depending, and then and there to be tried, wherein Joseph Blair is plaintiff, and James Marsh is defendant. And this you shall in no wise omit, under the penalty prescribed by law.

Witness, HM Houston, Clerk of our said Court, at Office the 6th Monday after the 4th Monday in March and in the seventy 6th year of our Independence, A.D. 1852. Issued Oct. 14th, 1852.
HM Houston Clk

Joseph Blair Vs James Marsh
Subpoena for Dft.
J.U. Griffin

To Fall Term, 1852
Executed, D. Rushing, Shff

State of North Carolina.
To the Sheriff of Union County, Greeting:
You are hereby commanded to Summon J. U. Griffin personally to be and appear before the Judges of our Superior Court of Law, at the next Court to be held for our said County, at the Court House in Monroe on the 6th Monday after the 4th Monday in September next, then and there to testify and the truth to say, in behalf of James Marsh in a certain matter of controversy before said Court depending, and then and there to be tried, wherein Joseph Blair is plaintiff, and James Marsh is defendant. And this you shall in no wise omit, under the penalty prescribed by law.

Witness, HM Houston, Clerk of our said Court, at Office the 6th Monday after the 4th Monday in March, and in the seventy 6th year of our Independence, A.D. 1852. Issued Oct. 14th, 1852.
HM Houston Clk

Joseph Blair Vs James Marsh
Subp for Pltff
John Walden
To Fall Term 1852
Executed, D. Rushing, Shff

State of North Carolina.
To the Sheriff of Union County, Greeting:

You are hereby commanded to Summon John Walden personally to be and appear before the Judges of our Superior Court of Law, at the next Court to be held for our said county, at the Court House in Monroe on the 6th Monday after the 4th Monday in September next, then and there to testify and the truth to say, in behalf of Joseph Blair in a certain matter of controversy before said Court depending, and then and there to be tried, wherein Joseph Blair is plaintiff, and James Marsh is defendant. And this you shall in no wise omit, under the penalty prescribed by law.

Witness, HM Houston, Clerk of our said Court, at Office the 6th Monday after the 4th Monday in March, and in the seventy 6th year of our Independence, A.D. 1852.
HM Houston CSC

Joseph Blair vs James Marsh
Subpoena for Pltff
John King
To Fall Term 1852
Executed, D. Rushing, Shff

State of North Carolina.
To the Sheriff of Union County, Greeting:

Your are hereby commanded to Summon John King personally to be and appear before the Judges of our Superior Court of Law, at the next Court to be held for our said county, at the Court House in Monroe on the 6th Monday after the 4th Monday in September next, then and there to testify and the truth to say, in behalf of Joseph Blair in a certain matter of controversy before said Court depending, and then and there to be tried, wherein Joseph Blair is plaintiff, and James Marsh is defendant. And this you shall in no wise omit, under the penalty prescribed by law.

Witness, HM Houston, Clerk of our said Court, at Office, the 6th Monday after the 4th Monday in March and in the seventy 6th year of our Independence, A.D. 1852.
HM Houston CSC

Joseph Blair vs James Marsh
Subp for Pltff
Sarah Stack
To Fall Term 1852
Executed, D. Rushing, Shff

State of North Carolina.
To the Sheriff of Union County, Greeting:
You are hereby commanded to Summon Sarah Stack personally to be and appear before the Judge of our Superior Court of Law, at the next Court to be held for our said county, at the Court House in Monroe on the 6th Monday after the 4th Monday in September next, then and there to testify, and the truth to say, in behalf of Joseph Blair in a certain matter of controversy before said Court depending, and then and there to be tried,

wherein Joseph Blair is plaintiff, and James Marsh is defendant. And this you shall in no wise omit, under the penalty prescribed by law.

Witness, HM Houston, Clerk of our said Court, at Office, the 6th Monday after the 4th Monday in March, and in the seventy 6th year of our Independence, A.D. 1852.
HM Houston CSC

Joseph Blair vs James Marsh
Subp for Pltff
Archibald Marsh
To Fall Term 1852
Executed, D. Rushing, Shff

State of North Carolina.
To the Sheriff of Union County, Greeting:

You are hereby commanded to Summon Archibald Marsh personally to be and appear before the Judge of our Superior Court of Law, at the next Court to be held for our said County, at the Court House in Monroe on the 6th Monday after the 4th Monday in Sept. next, then and there to testify, and the truth to say, in behalf of Joseph Blair in a certain matter of controversy before said Court depending, and then and there to be tried, wherein Joseph Blair is plaintiff, and James Marsh is defendant. And this you shall in no wise omit, under the penalty prescribed by law.

Witness, HM Houston, Clerk of our said Court, at Office the 6th Monday after the 4th Monday in March and in the seventy 6th year of our Independence.
H.M. Houston CSC

Joseph Blair vs James Marsh
Sub for Pltff
William King
To Fall Term 1852
Executed, D. Rushing, Shff

State of North Carolina.
To the Sheriff of Union County, greeting:

You are hereby commanded to Summon William King personally to be and appear before the Judge of our Superior Court of Law, at the next Court to be held for our said county, at the Court House in Monroe on the 6th Monday after the 4th Monday in September next, then and there to testify, and the truth to say, in behalf of Joseph Blair in a certain matter of controversy before said Court depending, and then and there to be tried, **wherein Joseph Blair is plaintiff, and James Marsh is defendant. And this** you shall in no wise omit, under the penalty prescribed by law.

Witness, H.M. Houston Clerk of our said Court, at Office, the 6th Monday after the 4th Monday in March, and in the seventy 6th year of our Independence, A.D. 1852.
HM Houston CSC

Joseph Blair vs James Marsh
Sup for Plaintiff
Thos. L. Marsh
To Fall Term 1852
Executed, D. Rushing, Shff

State of North Carolina.
To the Sheriff of Union County, Greeting:

You are hereby commanded to Summon Thos. L. Marsh personally to be and appear before the Judges of our Superior Court of Law, at the next Court to be held for our said county, at the Court House in Monroe on the 6th Monday after the 4th Monday in September next, then and there to tesrify, and the truth to say, in behalf of Joseph Blair in a certain matter of controversy before said Court depending, and then and there to be tried, wherein Joseph Blair is plaintiff, and James Marsh is defendant. And this you shall in no wise omit, under the penalty prescribed by law.

Witness, HM Houston Clerk of our said Court, at Office, the 6th Monday after the 4th Monday in March, and in the seventy 6th year of our Independence, A.D. 1852.
HM Houston CSC

Joseph Blair vs James Marsh
Subp for Pltff

Thomas Huntley
To Fall Term 1852
Executed, D. Rushing, Shff

State of North Carolina.
To the Sheriff of Union County, Greeting:
You are hereby commanded to Summon Thos. Huntley personally to be and appear before the Judge of our Superior Court of Law, at the next Court to be held for our said county, at the Court House in Monroe on the 6th Monday after the 4th Monday in September next, then and there to testify, and the truth to say, in behalf of Joseph Blair in a certain matter of controversy before said Court depending, and then and there to be tried, wherein Joseph Blair is plaintiff, and James Marsh is defendant. And this you shall in no wise omit, under the penalty prescribed by law.

Witness, HM Houston Clerk of our said Court at Office, the 6th Monday after the 4th Monday in March, and in the seventy 6th year of our Independence, A.D. 1852.
H.M. Houston CSC

Joseph Blair vs James Marsh
HM Houston, Clerk of Superior Court
Opened by HM Houston
Union County, Monroe -- No Ca.

Joseph Blair } Superior Court
vs } Union County
James Marsh } North Carolina

Dr. Richard E Wylie Says he is acquainted with the Plaintiff, but does not know the Defendant, Says he examined a negro Boy named Lewis carefully & thoroughly, belonging to the Plaintiff and found him labouring under incurable organic disease of the heart, which disease was unquestionably, of long standing, and in the opinion of the witness, he has no doubt, that it had an existence for ten or fifteen years, perhaps longer, The Witness states that he first examined the Negro in 1851, & Again in the summer of 1852 - he made for the Negro no medical prescription whatever, for that he looked upon the Case as hopelessly incurable - he may have given some directions to the Plaintiff what to do in order to

prolong his life, but he never took the Negro as a Patient and never made any charge against the Plaintiff - Witness would regard the Negro as a charge upon any Mans hands, and Worse than Worthless - Witness is a regular practising Physician and has been so for the last twenty years - the Witness fully tested the ability of the Negro to endure labour and found him unable to walk up a hill, use an axe or hoc without great difficulty of breathing - The witness States that Convulsions, great pain in the breast and arms attended with a cramp are some of the Symptoms that Patients labouring under this particular disease of the heart may be expected to have - The Technical name of the disease under which the Negro laboured is Hypertrophy of the heart
R.E. Wylie

Joseph Blair } Superior Court
vs } Union County
James Marsh } No Carolina

I John Williams, Magistrate for Lancaster District in pursuance of the constructions of a Commission to me directed in the above case do hereby certify that I have caused Dr RE Wylie to come before me in my office at Lancaster Court House South Carolina on Monday the first day of November 1852, and have examined him in and about the matter of controversy, now at Issue in the above case, and that the foregoing is the examination and deposition of the witness Dr Richard E. Wylic by me taken this 1st Nov. 1852.
John Williams (LS)
Magistrate

Joseph Blair } Superior Court
vs }
James Marsh } Union County, N.C.

Commissioners fee for takeing examination of Dr RE Wylie by Comms in the above case. $5.00
John Williams, Magistrate

Joseph Blair vs James Marsh
Pros Bond

State of North Carolina.
Supr. Court Office, Union County

We, the subscribers, do jointly and severally bind ourselves, our heirs, executors ans administrators, in the sum of Two hundred Dollars to James Marsh his heirs, executors, administrators and assigns. The obligation to be void on condition that Joseph Blair do prosecute a certain suit, brought in the Court aforesaid, by Joseph Blair against James Marsh and in case of failure, shall pay the said James Marsh such costs and damages as may be awarded against the said him by the Court having cognizance thereof. Witness our hands and seals, the 3rd day of Nov. 1852.

Witness	Joseph Blair	(Seal)
A Little	JM Sehorn[?]	(Seal)

Chapter Twelve

Union County

Sales of Slaves

[No Date.]

Sales of Negroes

Boy George bidd off by Wm. P. Robinson for the Sum of	$780
Boy Byer bidd off by Wm. P. Robinson for the Sum of	$850
Girl Sindy bid of by **[Blank]** for the Sum of	**[Blank]**
Boy Joe bidd off by Wm. P. Robinson at the Sum of	$600
	2230
Boy Isaac bidd off by **[Blank]** at the Sum of	**[Blank]**
Boy Leas bidd off by **[Blank]** at the Sum of	**[Blank]**
Boy Amos bidd of by **[Blank]** at the Sum of	**[Blank]**
Rene & Child Tom bid off by **[Faded]** at the Sum of	**[Blank]**
Rene & Isaac & Amos & Tom bidd of by Wm. P. Robinson	$1500
	$3730

Chapter Thirteen

Union County

Division of Slaves

Report of Commiss. in Partition for
William & Susan Marsh & Others
Return This File to Box No. 44

State of North Carolina } 31st Nov. 1860 This Report was duly
Union County } Registered in the Registers office Book

No. 5 page 168 **[768?]** J.F. McLure, Register

State of North Carolina }
Union County }

We the undersigned freeholders appointed by the Court of pleas and quarter Sessions of Said County having been duly Sworn proceeded on the 31st day of January 1860 to divide and make partition between and among Susan Marsh, William Marsh, Sarah Marsh, Frank Marsh, Mary V Marsh & Elisha Marsh tenants in Common of Certain value property and alloted and assign to each his and her share in severalty as follows that is to say

Joe valued at	1300
Sack	1100
Sally	1000
Dinah	1000
Isham	1050
Henry	900
Valuation	6350

Alloted Joe to Susan Marsh at Thirteen hundred Dollars in severalty and Sack, Sally, Dinah, Isham **[Torn]** Henry to William Marsh, Sarah Marsh, Frank Marsh, Mary V Marsh & Elisha Marsh at Five Thousand and Fifty Dollars in Common, Joe being Two hundred and Forty one Dollars and Sixty seven cents moore than Susan Marsh Shear in the negros wich Sum she will pay over to William Marsh, Sarah Marsh, Frank Marsh, Mary V Marsh & Elisha Marsh in Common.

All of wich is Respectfully submited under our hands and seals this 31 of January 1860.

BC Ashcraft (Seal)
[?] Ashcraft (Seal)
John Ashcraft (Seal)

for wich services to Comisners Clames pay for One day Each.

****

Abner C. Houston & Mary Jane Houston
by Jane Houston guardn.
Petition Division Slaves
To July Term 1858

Robt G. Howard, Jas. H. Morrison & Thos. G. Ezzel
Walkup, Atto.

State of North Carolina } Court of Pleas & Quarter Sessions
Union County } July Term 1858

To the Worshipful the Justices of said Court.

The Petition of Abner C. Houston of full age & Mary J. Houston a Minor under age by her guardian Jane Houston, respectfully showeth unto your Worships that they are tenants in Common of the following Slaves, towit Elias, Adaline, Isaac, Judah & Hetta, Your petitioners further show that they wish to have the said Slaves divided between them & that they may hold their shares in severalty, to that end they pray your Worships to appoint three freeholders unconnected with them by consanguinity or affinity, to divide the said slaves into two equall parts &

shares & to allot & set apart to each your petitioners one of said Shares in severalty, & to report their proceedings in due form of law to the next Term of this Court. And Your petitioners as in duty bound will ever Pray. S.H. Walkup, Atto. for petrs.

Abner C. Houston } To July Term 1858
Mary Jane Houston by }
Jane Houston Guardn. }Petition for Division
Ex Parte } of Slaves

The Commissioners who were appointed at last Term of this Court, to divide the Slaves named in the petition [?] the parties, having filed their report during the present term, And the division made by them appearing to the satisfaction of the Court to be fair & equal, the said report is in all respects confirmed & ordered to be recorded, & it is ordered & adjudged that the Parties pay the costs proportionably.

Abner C. Houston & } To July Term 1858
Mary J. Houston Ex Parte } Order appointing Commissioners

On Motion the following freeholders to wit, Robt. G. Howard, Jas. H. Morrison & Thos. G. Ezzell are appointed commissioners to divide the slaves named in the petition into two equal parts & shares & allot to each of the petitioners one Share thereof in severalty, & to report their proceedings in due form of law to the next Term of this Court.

****

James F. Hill & Wife & Others
Ex Parte
Petition to Sell Negroes
To Fall Term 1856
Wilson, Atto

State of North Carolina } Superior Court of Law
Union County } Fall Term 1856

To the Honorable the Judge of the Superior Court of Law for the County & State aforesaid.

The Petition of James F. Hill & Martha his Wife & William H. Simpson, of full age, and John M. Harrison, June Harrison, Eleazer Harrison and Amanda Harrison, infants, who Sue their Guardian A.H. Crowell, respectfully represent to your Honor that your Petitioners are owners as Tenants in Common of the following Negroes, Tolbis, Susan & her two children June & Margaret, being three in number - That your Petitioners Hill & wife Martha are Entitled to one individual Sixth part thereof, your Petitioner Simpson to one individual Sixth Part, and your infant Petitioners, even to one individual Sixth part - That in order to make a division of sd. Negroes it is necessary that they should be sold - Your Petitioners therefore pray your Honor to order a Decree that sd. Negroes be sold, upon Such Terms as to your Honor shall seem reasonable, and the proceeds thereof be divided among them in accordance with their respective rights - And Your Petitioners as in duty bound will ever pray.
Wilson, Atto

In the matter of James F. Hill & Wife & Others

This case coming on to be heard upon the proceedings of the petitioners, the Court declares it's opinion thereon to be that the order to make a division of the Slaves in the proceedings mentioned that it is necessary, That sd. Negroes should be Sold.

It is thereupon ordered & Decreed by the Court that William H. Simpson be appointed a Commissioner of this Court to Sell sd. Slaves at Public Auction at the Court House in Monroe, upon a credit of Six Months with interest after having advertised the same in conformity to Law, taking Bonds with approved Security for the purchase money, and that he make a report of his proceedings to next Court.

State of North Carolina } Superior Court of Law
Union County } Spring Term 1857

James F Hill & Wife & Others, Petition to sell Negroes

In this Case it is ordered and decreed by the Court that Wm H Simpson Clerk be appointed a Commissioner of this Court to Sell said Slaves at public auction at the Court house in Monroe upon a credit of Six Months with Interest after having advertised in conformity to Law taking Bond with approved Security for the purchase Money.

There fore I WH Simpson Commissioner as aforesaid do hereby Certify that I advertised the said Negroes Mentioned in the pleadings of the Petitioners at the Court house door in Monroe, Union County, and at three & Moor other public places in Said County in conformity with the Law and proceeded to Sell the Same at the Court house door in Monroe on the 7th day of April 1857 at Which time and place John Medlin be came the Last and highest bidder at the Sum of Seventeen hundred and Eighty Six dollars who entered into bond & Security for the same Which was approved with Interest from date.

And I further Certify that I believe said Negroes Sold for a Valuable consideration, All of Which is Respectfully Reported to your Honr.

Wm. H. Simpson, Commr.

James F. Hill & Wife and Others, ExParte
Petition to Sell Negroes
Commissioners Report
To Spring Term 1857

In the matter of James F. Hill & Wife & Others

This Case coming on for further consideration on the Report of Mr. Wm. H. Simpson, Commissioner, and is appearing therefore that the negroes sold for a fair price, it is ordered by by the Court that the same be confirmed.

It is further ordered that the Commissioner be allowed Twenty Dollars for his services in making the Sale, and distributing the money among the tenants in Common.

It is further ordered that the Costs of this Suit, meaning the allowance to the Commissioner, to be Taxed by the Clerk & paid out of the Fund.

It is furthered ordered that this Decree be Enrolled.

****

Archy M Larty guardn. of Martha M Larty & Thos. A. M Larty
Exparte, Petition Division of Slaves
To October term 1856
Walkup, Atto.

State of North Carolina } Court of Pleas & Quarter Sessions
Union County } Octr. term 1856

To the Worshipful the Justices of said Court.

The petition of Thomas Alexr. McLarty & of Martha A. McLarty as person non Compus Mentis who sues by her next friend & guardian & the guardian of both the aforesaid, Archibald McLarty, respectfully sheweth unto your Worships that the said Thos. A. McLarty & Martha A. Mclarty are tenants in Common of the following negroes to wit, Rose, Henry, Ralph, Amelia, Margaret, Sandy, Napoleon, Isaac, Ann & Jasper.

Your Petitioners further show that they desire to hold their shares of said Slaves in severalty & to that end they pray your Worships to appoint three freeholders unconnected with them by Consanguinity or affinity to divide the said Slaves into three equal parts & shares, & to allot & set apart to each of Your petitioners one of said Shares in severalty & to report their proceedings in due form of law to the next term of this Court.

And your petitioners as in duty bound will ever pray.
S.H. Walkup, Atto. for Petitioners.

State of North Carolina }
Union County } October Term 1856

Ordered by the Court that Hugh M Houston, C. Austin, & D.A. Covington be and they are hereby Appointed Commissioners to make Partition of the Slaves belonging to Tho A McLarty & Martha Mclarty, and make report to next term of this Court, 8th Decr. 1856
JM Stewart Clk.

Partition of the Slaves Between Thos. A. McLarty & Martha McLarty
To Jany Term 1857

HM Houston }
C Austin } Commissioners
DA Covington }

State of North Carolina }
Union County }

In obedience to the Annexed Order from the County Court. We the undersigned Commissioners, at the House of A. McLarty on Monday the 22d. December 1856, proceeded to allot and make partition of the Slaves belonging to Thomas A. McLarty, and his sister Martha McLarty. And found the Slaves to be ten in number [?] aged and Valued as follows towit.

1. Rose	aged about 39 years	Valuation	550.00
2. Henry	20 years & 9 Months		900.00
3. Ralf	18 years & 6 Months		1100.00
4. Amelia	15 years & 6 Months		850.00
5. Margarett	12 years & 6 Months		900.00
6. Sandy	10 years & 10 Months		750.00
7. Napoleon	9 years & 6 Months		700.00
8. Isaac	6 years & 2 Months		550.00
9. Ann	4 years & 3 Months		550.00
10. Jasper	3 years & 3 Months		350.00
			7200.00

(Seven Thousand & Two Hundred Dollars)

Lot No. 1	Rose	550	Lot No. 2	Henry	900
	Ralf	1100		Margarett	900
	Amelia	850		Napoleon	700
	Jasper	350		Isaac	550
	Sandy	750		Ann	550
		3600			3600

That Two lots equal in valuation and each valued at Three Thousand and Six Hundred Dollars, Lot No. 1 was drawn for Martha McLarty. And Lot

No. 2 for Thomas McLarty. Respectfully submitted to the Worshipful Court at January Term 1857.

D.A. Covington }
H.M. Houston } Commissioners
C. Austin }

Glossary of Legal Terms

[Definitions of legal terms appearing in transcriptions within this book are derived from *Black's Law Dictionary*. See footnote below]

Slave: An individual who has no freedom and is subject to another in whole. His person and services are completely under the control of another. He belongs to his Master, and his industry and labor are not his own. His Master may sell or dispose of his person.

Referee: An individual who is referred by the court in a cause pending to listen to the testimony and parties involved and return a report to the court.

Guarnished: A furnishing or garnishment.

Attachment: The legal seizing of someones property to comply with a writ or judicial order to satisfy a judgment not yet rendered.

Forma Pauperis: A provision made for a poor person to have their day in court without liability for fees or costs.

Non Compus Mentis: Incompetent , or not of a sound mind.

Next Friend: An individual who acts for the benefit of an infant; or a person who is not able to look after his own business or interests. It is similar to Guardian Ad Litem.

Tenants in Common: Tenants who hold the same property (including slaves) together by several and distinct titles.

Glossary of Legal Terms

Severalty: Individuals who own real or personal property without other persons sharing in the ownership

A & B (Assault & Battery): Unlawful touching of another individual without excuse or justification.

Guardian: An individual invested with power for caring for someone who is incapable of handling their own affairs.

Ne Exeat: A writ that forbids an individual to flee the country, state or jurisdiction of the court.

Testamentary Trustee: An individual chosen or appointed to fulfill or carry out a trust created by a will.

Trustee: An individual who is chosen or appointed by law to execute a trust.

Hue & Cry: A loud outcry to pursue felons (robbers and murderers) , and all who heard it were bound to join in the pursuit.

Outlaw: In English law, an individual who has been banned from the protection of the law.

Habeas Corpus: A writ commonly directed to a sheriff ordering him to deliver a prisoner, or an individual who is to be detained. The purpose is to test the legality of the detention, and not whether the individual is guilty or innocent.

Writ: A judicial order that is written for a specific act, or giving power to another to have it done.

Replevin: A legal action giving the owner or person entitled the right to repossession of property from someone who has wrongfully taken or detains his property.

Inquest: An inquisition by a Coroner, sometimes accompanied by a jury to investigate the death of someone who has been killed, or died under suspicious circumstances.

Tax District: A district to which a tax is ratably apportioned, and levied upon its population.

Injunction: A court order prohibiting an individual from committing a certain act, or ordering an individual to undo an injury.[6]

[6] Henry Campbell Black, M.A., *Black's Law Dictionary*, 6th ed. (St. Paul, Minn.: West Publishing Company, 1990)

Index and Table of Cases

Cases

Index and Table of Cases

Index and Table of Cases

Index and Table of Cases

Index and Table of Cases

A

Index and Table of Cases

N

Q

T

ABOUT THE AUTHORS

WILLIAM L. BYRD, III has been involved in genealogical and historical research for more than thirty years. His primary areas of interest are Native Americans, African Americans, West Indians, East Indians and Moors in Virginia, North Carolina, and South Carolina.

He has been published by the *North Carolina Genealogical Society Journal*, the *Magazine of Virginia Genealogy*, *The Rowan County Register*, and *The South Carolina Magazine of Ancestral Research*. He has also co-authored articles with Sheila Stover in the *North Carolina Genealogical Society Journal*, *The Augustan Society Omnibus*, the *Pan-American Indian Association News*, and the *Eagle: New England's American Indian Journal*. He has received an "Award of Special Recognition" from The North Carolina Society of Historians in the category of "The History Article Award" for preserving North Carolina history.

He is a U.S. Army Veteran from the Vietnam era, and served with the U.S. Armed Forces overseas. He is currently retired, and resides with his family in Hickory, North Carolina.

☙ ❧

JOHN H. SMITH holds a BA in psychology from Lenoir Rhyne College, and did his graduate work at Winthrop University. His professional memberships include American Psychological Association, and Phi Alpha Theta (National Honor Society in History.) In addition to his full-time career, Mr. Smith is a part-time continuing education instructor of genealogy and family history, and a part-time research assistant to Catawba County Historical Association.

Mr. Smith was the editor of *The Burke Journal* (1992-1995), a quarterly publication of the Burke County Genealogical Society, (winner of the *Excellence in Periodical Publishing Award* from the North Carolina Genealogical Society, 1995.) He has presented numerous programs to genealogical groups in North Carolina in the past fifteen years, and has twice been a speaker at the South Carolina Genealogical Society's summer workshop. His articles have been published in *The Burke Journal*, *Catawba Cousins*, the *Rowan Register*, the *South Carolina Magazine of Ancestral Research* and several other local/county quarterlies.

Other Heritage Books by William L. Byrd, III:

Against the Peace and Dignity of the State: North Carolina Laws Regarding Slaves, Free Persons of Color, and Indians

Bladen County, North Carolina Tax Lists: 1768 through 1774, Volume I

Bladen County, North Carolina Tax Lists: 1775 through 1789, Volume II

For So Long as the Sun and Moon Endure: Indian Records from the North Carolina General Assembly Sessions, & Other Sources

In Full Force and Virtue: North Carolina Emancipation Records, 1713-1860

North Carolina General Assembly Sessions Records: Slaves and Free Persons of Color, 1709-1789

North Carolina Slaves and Free Persons of Color: Chowan County, Volume One

North Carolina Slaves and Free Persons of Color: Chowan County, Volume Two

North Carolina Slaves and Free Persons of Color: Pasquotank County

North Carolina Slaves and Free Persons of Color: Perquimans County

Villainy Often Goes Unpunished: Indian Records from the North Carolina General Assembly Sessions, 1675-1789

Other Heritage Books by William L. Byrd, III and John H. Smith:

North Carolina Slaves and Free Persons of Color: Burke, Lincoln, and Rowan Counties

North Carolina Slaves and Free Persons of Color: Hyde and Beaufort Counties

North Carolina Slaves and Free Persons of Color: Iredell County

North Carolina Slaves and Free Persons of Color: Mecklenburg, Gaston, and Union Counties

North Carolina Slaves and Free Persons of Color: McDowell County

North Carolina Slaves and Free Persons of Color: Stokes and Yadkin Counties

www.ingramcontent.com/pod-product-compliance
Lightning Source LLC
LaVergne TN
LVHW050616100826
845148LV00011B/1612

* 9 7 8 0 7 8 8 4 1 8 5 1 8 *